They Kept the Lower Lights Burning:

The Story of the Seaman's Bethel at Martha's Vineyard, Massachusetts, and it Chaplains

by

George W. Wiseman

First Fruits Press
Wilmore, Kentucky
c2012

ISBN: 9781621710202

They Kept the Lower Lights Burning: The Story of the Seaman's Bethel at Martha's Vineyard, Massachusetts, and its Chaplains, by George William Wiseman.
First Fruits Press, © 2012
Previously published by the author in 1978.

Digital version at http://place.asburyseminary.edu/firstfruitsbooks/4/

First Fruits Press is a digital imprint of the Asbury Theological Seminary, B.L. Fisher Library. Asbury Theological Seminary is the legal owner of the material previously published by the Pentecostal Publishing Co. and reserves the right to release new editions of this material as well as new material produced by Asbury Theological Seminary. Its publications are available for noncommercial and educational uses, such as research, teaching and private study. First Fruits Press has licensed the digital version of this work under the Creative Commons Attribution Noncommercial 3.0 United States License. To view a copy of this license, visit http://creativecommons.org/licenses/by-nc/3.0/us/.

For all other uses, contact:

First Fruits Press
B.L. Fisher Library
Asbury Theological Seminary
204 N. Lexington Ave.
Wilmore, KY 40390
http://place.asburyseminary.edu/firstfruits

Wiseman, George W.
　They kept the lower lights burning : the story of the Seaman's Bethel at Martha's Vineyard, Massachusetts, and its chaplains / George William Wiseman.
　Wilmore, Ky. : First Fruits Press, c2012.
　196 p. : ill., ports. ; 21 cm.
　Reprint. Previously published: Bradenton, Fla. : Wiseman, 1978.
　ISBN: 9781621710202 (pbk.)
　1. Merchant mariners -- Missions and charities -- Massachusetts -- Martha's Vineyard. 2. Martha's Vineyard (Mass.) -- History. I. Title.
　BV2675.M377 W572012　　　　　　　　　　　　　　　266/.009744/94

Cover design by Haley Hill

asburyseminary.edu
800.2ASBURY
204 North Lexington Avenue
Wilmore, Kentucky 40390

THEY KEPT THE LOWER LIGHTS BURNING

The story of the Seaman's Bethel at Martha's Vineyard, Massachusetts, and its Chaplains.

George William Wiseman

Published By
GEORGE W. WISEMAN
Rt. 1, Box 279, Res. 56
Bradenton, Fla. 33508

© Copyright By
George W. Wiseman

Printed By
DANIELS PUBLISHERS
1209 29th Street
Orlando, Florida, 32805

To the memory of

CHAPLAIN MADISON EDWARDS and his dedicated wife MARY ELLA; and CHAPLAIN AUSTIN TOWER and his devoted wife HELEN—who kept the lights burning for the seamen of Vineyard Sound for nearly 80 years.

CONTENTS

Foreword ... ix

Chapter One
Thus Passed the Seaman's Friend ... 13

Chapter Two
A Missionary is Born ... 18

Chapter Three
A Lonely Journey ... 24

Chapter Four
Boston Makes a Discovery ... 29

Chapter Five
The Floating Christian Endeavor ... 35

Chapter Six
The Allure of Martha's Vineyard ... 40

Chapter Seven
The Promised Land at Last ... 43

Chapter Eight
The Fury of the Storm ... 47

Chapter Nine
Another Dedication; Another Storm ... 52

Chapter Ten
Tears of Sadness and Joy ... 56

Chapter Eleven
The Portland Storm ... 59

Chapter Twelve
God's Acre ... 69

Chapter Thirteen
A Colorful Parade of Helpers ... 76

Chapter Fourteen
Turn of the Century   80

Chapter Fifteen
A Second Missionary Emerges   85

Chapter Sixteen
Comfort for the Sailor   89

Chapter Seventeen
The Dangers of Ice   94

Chapter Eighteen
The Hold Fast Brotherhood   99

Chapter Nineteen
Story of the Aransas   104

Chapter Twenty
The Bethel Expands   108

Chapter Twenty-One
Wedding Bells, A Lighthouse and Some Problems   112

Chapter Twenty-Two
All Hands on Deck   119

Chapter Twenty-Three
The Caruso of the Bowery   125

Chapter Twenty-Four
The Story of Richard Halstead   131

Chapter Twenty-Five
The Gospel Skippers   134

Chapter Twenty-Six
A Night at the Bethel   139

Chapter Twenty-Seven
Shipmates at Rest   146

Chapter Twenty-Eight
Drama of Peace and War   149

Chapter Twenty-Nine
Captain Edwards Has Gone Aloft   155

Chapter Thirty
A Wanderer   158

Chapter Thirty-One
A New Launch and Another Explosion   162

Chapter Thirty-Two
A Noble Daughter of the Vineyard   166

Chapter Thirty-Three
A Life of Compassion and Love   171

Chapter Thirty-Four
Homeward Bound   180

Chapter Thirty-Five
The End of an Era   184

Afterword   188

Acknowledgements   191

The Seamen's Cemeteries   192

Names in the Bethel Cemetery Lot   193

Names in the Marine Hospital Cemetery   195

FOREWORD

The Bay of Fundy was blanketed with fog. On a morning when the fog had been particularly heavy, the news of a vessel wrecked on the Western Head echoed and reechoed through the village. The fishing boats were already on their way to save lives or salvage whatever was available. A vacationing minister[1] joined those hurrying along the shore, as anxious as they to reach the wreck. Soon the rendezvous was reached and the tragedy was immediately apparent to all. The vessel lay head-in on the shore. Her bowsprit over-reached the cliffs, and her stern still remained in the murky sea. She was being mercilessly pounded by the surf, and looking upon her one knew she would probably never sail again.

The most pathetic figure was the captain, sitting upon a rock surrounded by a few articles he was able to save, and looking at the tragic plight of the vessel that had long been his home. At his feet were his precious instruments, his money box and a few other valuables he was able to take with him when he climbed, by way of the bowsprit chains, to the shore.

As the minister drew closer in an attempt to comfort him, his eye caught a book that lay among the disordered articles at his feet. It was water stained and torn, but the captain must have considered it of great value to be among the few things worthy to be saved. Looking closer, he noticed it was a Bible, and stooping, picked it up. Glancing inside he read these simple words: "Presented by the Vineyard Haven Bethel of the Boston Seaman's Friend Society." Beneath the inscription, written in large letters, was the Captain's name. While anchored in Vineyard Haven harbor, perhaps many years before, this captain of the "Addie Fuller" visited the Bethel to see his old friend Chaplain Madison Edwards, and before leaving received the Bible, now laying in disarray upon the shore.

What happened in the thick fog the night before, might

never be fully explained. But something went wrong, for instead of the open channel, the vessel ran amidst the breakers and struck upon the sand. When it came to saving his valuables his Bible was among them—a gift from the man who had led him, like hundreds of other seamen, to value those things that are eternal.

This is the story of that chaplain, Madison Edwards, and also Chaplain Austin Tower of the Seamen's Bethel at Vineyard Haven, Massachusetts. No two men ever made the Bible more meaningful to seamen than these devoted servants, even though thousands of others, through the years, dedicated their lives to that end.

The education of both chaplains was limited, their training for the work insufficient and their income meager. However, this lack was compensated for by an overwhelming passion for the men of the sea, and the rare ability to convey their love and concern. Every newcomer soon became aware that in each chaplain they had a friend who would stand by them. They also quickly sensed that the Christ they were urged to follow lived in the lives of these spiritual leaders, and that made them want this Divine Pilot, too. More conversions took place in that little "House of God" than in any church of their day. The first concern of both chaplains was with the bodily needs of men, but the lasting concern was with their soul.

They were both blessed with helpmates who were as anxious for the well-being of the seamen as they were. Their lives were always an inspiration and an example. This history will tell also of these noble women and their part in the Bethel work.

This is more than a history of the Bethel and its chaplains. It is also a story of a few of the many seamen, who found a more radiant life in the religious atmosphere that pervaded the chapel, but left to enter the shadows of tragedy at sea.

Because this book deals with the Seamen's Bethel in Vineyard Haven, let it not be assumed that the self-sacrificing ministry of the host of faithful workers in Boston and other seaport cities throughout the world, have been forgotten. Actually, this is their story, too.

In Joel 2:28, God said, "I will pour out my Spirit upon all flesh; and your sons and daughters shall prophesy, your old men shall dream dreams, and your young men shall see visions." This prophesy has been fulfilled in our generation and multitudes the world over have become spirit-filled. However, God has never withheld His Spirit from individuals who have served Him faithfully through the ages. Among those who have been so blessed were the chaplains about whom this book is written.

George W. Wiseman

---

[1] Rev. Edward C. Boynton

Chapter One

"THUS PASSED THE SEAMAN'S FRIEND"

Clouds were scudding across the sky, indicating good sailing for the many small craft in the outer harbor of Vineyard Haven, Massachusetts. Vacationers were everywhere for this was the height of the summer season and that always meant happy, carefree, untroubled hours of rest or recreation. On this day, August 18, 1926, that joy was not in evidence in this seaport town, for the friend of seamen, Captain Madison Edwards, was to be buried at 2:00 p.m.

For fifty-eight years he had labored among the seamen of Vineyard Sound and thousands of sailors scattered throughout the world mourned him as they would one of their family.

Large numbers had arrived to attend the funeral rites. They represented every segment of society--rich and poor, summer visitors and townspeople. Among those present were members of the professions, including clergymen of all denominations. The seamen whom he loved, and who in turn loved him, were well represented, and mingling with the others were parents who had named a son after him. Perhaps even more important was the large number whom he had helped to get a new start in life. Two of these were to take part in the service.

The service was held in the Bethel filled with its thousand memories. It was there, in 1897, he moved his family to the newly furnished upstairs apartment. It was in this same assembly room in 1908 he saw his daughter, Helen, married to his young assistant, Austin Tower. The room was lined with flowers then, but on that occasion they were daises.

However, the real meaning of that place went far deeper. It had sacredness about it. It was here he quietly talked the wayward sailor into a new way of life or knelt in prayer with those who had just committed their lives to the Master through his tender persuasive ministry. It was in this room the "Hold Fast" brotherhood was organized, with its membership rules far more stringent than any church. And here he tenderly brought the bodies of those sailors who were to be buried in the Bethel lot, made all arrangements for their funeral services, and from here, followed them to the cemetery. In this room, hallowed by so many moving and touching experiences, he now was placed. This is where he wanted to be, the place he loved the most. Outside the flowers that he had carefully nurtured, bloomed in profusion, while inside many beautiful blossoms showed the love of friends.

The room filled rapidly as the appointed hour neared, and many gathered in small groups on the outside. The usual dockside noises were hushed, and someone remarked that even the seagulls were not as noisy as usual. Muffled sounds were heard as the people crowded into the Bethel, and family members were seated in the little office just a few feet away.

The office was small and rather crowded. It contained a good sized pigeonhole desk and a few small shelves containing his Bible, records, other books. Small family pictures, keepsakes and a large assortment of papers and letters filled the desk. Opposite was a bunk where the chaplain could rest or be handy on a stormy night, and above it, under glass, a display of photos and snapshots, mostly of seamen. A medicine cabinet and washbowl occupied the one vacant corner. Yet it was in this unpretentious room that, during his ministry, hundreds of seamen with personal, moral and spiritual problems too great too discuss openly, received encouragement, and knelt in prayer for a healing they never before had felt.

A simple service, befitting the life he led, followed. The Rev. Alfred Shelley, Chaplain of the Boston Seaman's Friend

Society, was in charge. The president, Rev. Samuel H. Woodrow, read the scripture and gave the opening prayer. Short but very meaningful eulogies were given by Rev. Merritt A. Farren and Rev. E. J. Curry, pastor of the Vineyard Haven Methodist Church. A solo was rendered by Miss Gonyon, and George Ellis who owed so much to Chaplain Edwards, and had travelled from New York to be present, sang two of the chaplains favorite hymns. A very touching prayer was offered by Rev. O. E. Denniston, pastor of the Bradley Memorial Church, Oak Bluffs, who had been encouraged by the chaplain, years before, to leave his home in Jamaica and come to Vineyard Haven.

There was a hush in the room during the many tributes that were paid, and one seaman, who had spent many years in the coastal trade, whispered, "Captain Edwards was a better father to me than my own has ever been."

After the benediction, those in the room, as well as those listening from the outside, filed by to look for the last time upon the one whom they had known, trusted and loved through the years. At this point strong men wept unashamedly for no one knew their loss better than the seamen.

S. S. Islander
with flag at half mast

During the service, the steamship "Islander" was docked at the wharf with her flag at half mast. When all had left, the deck hands and firemen of the steamship took their places to carry the casket aboard. All of them had been touched in some way by the goodness of this man, and they bore him quietly and reverently.

He was buried in the family lot in Woods Hole and many who attended the funeral left on the same boat for the service at the cemetery. When the shore was reached the same seamen carried the casket from the boat, whence it was borne to its final resting place.

Following is a touching tribute paid him at the time of his death.

Smooth is the sea and the sun sinks low,
Stilled is the storm king's blast,
Rippling soft in the sunset's glow
There flies the flag half mast.

Gone is the pilot who long stood by
Guiding with prayers and tears,
Toiling to aid when he heard the cry
Prompted by doubts and fears.

Calmly he sleeps, for his work is done,
Calmly he met the end;
When the Great Captain called home His son
Thus passed the seaman's friend.

Other hands now must take up his task,
Others must carry on –
Answering sadly, when seamen ask
"Where has our pilot gone?"

"Gone for a time from the ones he knew,
Angels above rejoice,
Since from the earth his great spirit flew,
Called by the Father's voice."

Thus passed the man who had been a towering source of strength throughout Vineyard Sound. In one of his New Year's messages he sent to his "boys" he wrote, "If this year shall bring to you the call of 'land ahead,' you may drop the anchor, furl the sail and be safe home at last."

Madison Edwards had dropped the anchor, furled the sail and was safe home at last.

Chapter Two

A MISSIONARY IS BORN

The year was 1868 and Madison Edwards had just turned sixteen. He had long been aware of the lack of concern shown seamen. He saw them walking the dusty roads of his town, lonely, many destitute, not knowing what to do or where to go, except to drinking places. He knew that many of them wanted a better place to spend their time when on shore leave. "No one cares for the sailor," he had said many times, "but I care and intend to help them."

Then an experience came that made this desire possible. He was attending a religious service at the Congregational

Madison Edwards at 16 when he boarded the Portland barque in Woods Hole 1868

Church in Falmouth, Massachusetts. Suddenly he began to tremble, as Paul must have done on the road to Damascus. He was convinced that he had received a Divine call to minister to seamen, and it was as real as though someone by his side had spoken to him. He had difficulty waiting until the service ended, he was so anxious to go home and plan how to answer that call. The answer was not long coming.

The next week he gathered a few of his close companions and rowed to a Portland barque anchored in the harbor of Woods Hole. Climbing aboard, he asked permission to hold a religous service. Captain and crew alike looked at him and his teenage assistants in amazement. Perhaps because of this unusual situation the captain gave an amused consent.

Madison didn't waste a moment. He led the crew in the singing of a few well known hymns, read a passage of Scripture, gave a short, down to earth talk, and ended with the only benediction he knew. Even the grinning sailors were quiet now. They seemed impressed, and when he left, shook his hand heartily and urged him to return when they anchored again. This was the beginning of fifty-eight years of the most fruitful work among seamen ever experienced along that section of our coast.

Madison Edwards was born in Woods Hole, Massachusetts, August 13, 1852, the son of Captain and Mrs. Benjamin Edwards. His ancestors were among the first to settle in this area. At the time of his birth, Woods Hole was a port of some consequence for sailing vessels, and thousands of them anchored there yearly.

His father was a well known captain, having been employed by the government on its first survey mission of Vineyard Sound and Nantucket Shoals in the 1850's. He was also the first commissioned buoy setter along the coast, a position he held for many years.

When Madison was born his father was captain of the buoy setter, "Active." In the same waters cruised Commodore Maxwell Woodhull of the United States Navy ship, "Madison" on a surveying mission. The two Captains were warm friends, and when the Edwards baby came, the Commodore hurried to offer his congratulations. Then he added, "If you will name him Madison for my ship, I'll give you fifty dollars for his education." After due consideration the offer was accepted and the baby was christened Madison.

The boy grew. He was exceedingly active and quick to notice things that went on around him. His playground was the harbor with its many boats. He came home repeatedly soaking wet. "I was born with seamen's blood in my veins," he once said, "and nothing was more soothing at night than the roar of the sea."

The next ten years were exciting but difficult. In order to continue he had to pay his own way. His field of labor covered many dangerous miles–forty two according to his own reckoning–yet he always returned home happy, but exhausted. He visited every vessel he could with fantastic results. Later, when he had a good launch, he intercepted every vessel going east or west and heaved aboard bundles of papers, magazines and religious tracts. He soon realized that the men needed a place on shore where they could meet, a room where they could gather for fellowship and sing the hymns learned in their hometown churches. With his parent's consent, he fitted up a room in his own home.

He knew many of them lacked something money could not buy. They needed to find themselves and a purpose for life that so far had eluded them. So he counselled with them, a mere youth often urging those twice his age to give up long standing habits he knew to be detrimental.

A few church groups gave small amounts to his work, and young people were willing to entertain, but for the next twenty years, Madison, with the help of his family would supply most of the money.

Soon the room in his home became too small, and he secured the use of a school house. He fixed it up to make it homelike and provide greater space for reading and writing materials.

In 1871, only three years after his first visit to a ship, a new hymn was written by P. P. Bliss, entitled, "Let the Lower Lights Be Burning." It was sung at the Moody-Sanky meetings and almost immediately became a popular request number in religious gatherings. Nowhere, however, was it sung with greater understanding and sincerity than where seamen gathered.

The next year when he was twenty, he bought his first boat, which was probably a sail boat. This made his visits to the vessels easier. A picture taken on his birthday show him with a mustache, which he kept through life, and receeding hair. His eyes could be described as having the penetrating, searching look that marked his successful ministry.

By 1878 Madison was very much in love. A young school teacher, Mary Ella Blandin, was living and teaching in the neighboring town of Falmouth, Massachusetts. They had met many times and talked of things they shared in common. This friendship had now turned into love for each other.

Her school picture, taken when she graduated from Wheaton Seminary, Norton, Massachusetts, in 1871, revealed, a keen, alive face, ready to meet life and challenge whatever problems might arise. She had a radiant, sunny disposition and possessed an inner beauty that one could not fail to notice. Although she was christened Mary, she was always called Ella.

She was genuinely religious and very understanding. "I do try in some ways to work for the Saviour," she wrote him, "But they seem so small. I am determined that my life may be more devoted to God and tonight I have consecrated myself again to Him to be engaged in His work, and I hope, a better Christian in all the days of the future. Pray for me when you can, and may God's richest blessing rest upon you and your work."

On Christmas day, 1880, he gave her a ring. It was not an engagement ring, but one that conveyed his love in a very tangible way. It was received in the same spirit. "I want to thank you ever and ever so much for the ring. It is very pretty. I never saw one like it. May I not have something, maybe a Bible verse, inside it that will help me?" she wrote. Apparently in the rush of their busy lives, it was put off and forgotten, for the ring, a most unusual one, is now in our possession and the inside is still blank.

In the meantime he was having problems of a different nature. Trouble developed at the Community Church in Woods Hole, called by everyone the "Hall." This was Liberty Hall where the Congregationalists worshipped. A liberal element had assumed the leadership and their program was distasteful to the orthodox. Consequently a split occured and Madison, due to his religious work to seamen, was right in the middle.

Those who opposed this "worldly trend" left the church and proceeded to organize their own. Madison was one of that number and consequently became the center of abuse. "I met a man tonight," he wrote, "who cursed me to my face. He called me all the mean things he could think of. He called me a liar and a hypocrite!" For a sensitive soul who never intended to do wrong, this caused a pain that remained with him for years. Madison and his conservative friends eventually organized the First Congregational Church of Woods Hole.

A few months previous to the wedding, Ella went to Fairhaven, Massachusetts, where she spent much time shopping in New Bedford, and with Madison, went house hunting. Time was running out, and they secured an upstairs apartment in haste. Madison went to look at it again the next week. What he discovered made him write immediately to Ella. "I went down the back stairs and I wish I could tell you how inconvenient it was. To get the coal we will have to go down two flights of stairs and get our wood we will have to go the same distance, and then through other rooms to the front cellar. It will be very hard to live there."

He had previously opened a shoe store in Fairhaven in order to earn enough to support a family. Ella was quite concerned and wrote, "Are you expecting to go to Danvers to learn what you need to know? I should think you would for there are so many different kinds of shoes just among ladies boots that I should think it would be puzzling for you."

Ella Blandin at the time of her marriage to Madison Edwards

Madison Edwards at the time of his marriage—1882

They were married as planned, April 26, 1882. He carried a small notebook in his pocket, and not long before the ceremony, perhaps when he was nervously pacing the floor, he wrote, "It is a solemn thing to be joined in Holy Matrimony." The next day the suspense had ended and he was his usual lighthearted self. That night they sat by their fire burning brightly on the hearth, and at the moment saw only a bright future before them.

Chapter Three

A LONELY JOURNEY

Their first year of marriage was not as anticipated. Two weeks after the wedding a very sick friend came to their home, asking if she could stay until she became well. The pleasant evenings by the hearth turned into long, dreary nights, while they stayed up many hours trying to ease their friends suffering.

On June 16 he sailed alone to Woods Hole. The sea was rough when he returned, and growing careless he fell overboard. It was an uncomfortable journey the rest of the way. If his bad luck ended there all would be well. However, in landing at his wharf in Fairhaven, he slipped and sprained his ankle. The next day it was so lame and sore he could barely step on it.

This should have been enough, but for him the worse trial was yet to come. Ella became seriously ill. The doctor described her illness as gastric fever and treated her the only way he knew how, but she grew steadily worse. For a month he wondered whether or not she would recover.

The fourth Sunday, however, marked a turning point. Having heard of a doctor in New Bedford, who had successfully treated this type of illness, he hurried to the city. To his surprise although it was Sunday, the doctor reached for his bag, and urging Madison to return home at once, said he would not be far behind. The next week Ella was sitting up and able to eat the food put before her.

Madison soon discovered that trouble was not easy to banish. Ella had just recovered when Fannie, a sister of Madison's, of whom he was very fond, was brought to the house. She had been sick for some time and in spite of medical attention she grew steadily worse. Their mother was no longer able to care for her, and Madison seemed to be the only hope. She would remain with them for a long time and was often so sick it was impossible to move her to change the bedding.

In the midst of this came a ray of sunshine. A healthy baby girl arrived on April 4, 1883 and both mother and baby did well. "We have dedicated her to the Lord at the beginning of this new life and relationship," he wrote on that day. She was named Helen Blandin.

Problems continued to plague the young couple, and their one source of joy was in little Helen and sometime later, the new arrival, Mary, whom they always called May.

They had long planned to move their shoe business to Woods Hole, and carpenters were busy building. In October the new home was nearly completed and Madison moved his family there. A store was also built for his shoe business, with a room set aside for the seamen he still served.

But something was wrong. For months he had felt the weight of unsatisfied longings. His promise to God was that he would spend his entire time ministering to seamen, yet in his endeavor to make a living he witnessed the constant erosion of that promised time.

In addition to his shoe store he had accepted the job of discharging coal and iron from vessels that arrived to unload. He hired a crew to work for him, and had to make enough money to pay his men and make a profit for himself. These two enterprises weighed heavily upon his conscience and caused him to feel that he was "smothering" the one desire he had at sixteen.

He had yet one more trial facing him before indecision could be put aside and he could commit his life fully to ministering to the men of the sea. In the early months of 1886, Madison went through a long, serious illness. It was however, during the most critical days of this affliction that the Lord again made known to him, His purpose for his life.

"I was to the border of the grave," he later wrote, "before I was willing to say 'yes' to the Lord. It was then I saw a white faced sailor boy standing before me, pleading with outstretched arms, and I said, 'I will give my life to this work.' " This was the second dedication of himself and it lasted until his death.

Now of primary importance was the regaining of health. For weeks he basked in the New England sunshine and sea air, but his lungs never ceased to hurt. Winter was fast approaching, and with his recovery still in doubt, it was decided he should go to Florida.

The first of December he left, in company of three other men, on a southbound steamer from Boston. The wind blew hard the first night of their trip, and increased in intensity the next day. The next night they were in the midst of a violent storm, described in one of his letters.

"At about 9:00 p.m. we passed close to the Scotland lightship where Lyman Norton is. After that we went to bed. The wind was blowing a perfect gale, making a terrible noise in the rigging. The vessel had her sails set to steady her. She was leaning down and rushing at a great speed. At 11:00 p.m., after I had been asleep, I was awakened by the stopping of the engines and immediately got up. We sprang to the window and saw a large three masted vessel coming right into us. You may be sure we left our room in a hurry and did not stop for clothes. I had on my drawers and socks. We ran to the deck. I got there just in time to see her strike us. She struck the fore rigging, and took off clean fifty feet of our rail and one boat. The stateroom next to ours where the stewardess stayed, was stove in. The steamer kept on her way and did not stop to see whether we had sunk the vessel or not. It was a narrow escape."

They continued without further incident and landed in Norfolk, Virginia, on December 4th. Madison had a steam launch ready for him there. He named her the Helen May, the first of three boats to be named after his little girls.

Florida was finally reached, and he made his way down the

St. Johns River, en route to Punta Gorda where he had planned to make his headquarters. He made arrangements to have his boat shipped by rail the remaining distance. The dock workers in handling the boat made a false move and the Helen May plunged stern first into the water, carrying with her food, bedding and clothing.

His next move was to sell the Helen May for $500.00 and invest in a partnership on a river steamer carrying mail and passengers. After a short period of apparent success, the partner took his share and left Madison with the boat. When he was finally able to sell her, he received only $150.00.

It was near the end of February. He had searched in vain for a means of livelihood that he might bring his family to Florida. Ella flatly refused. Loneliness had been a constant companion. "Oh, Ella," he wrote, "How I long to see you. I long to spend all my time home with you. Have my dear children forgotten me? I can't help shedding tears over this letter as I so much long to see you."

Pain was another companion that refused to leave him. "If it were not for the constant jeopardy of my old complaint," he wrote Ella, "I could stand it, but it comes so suddenly on me. If I had diseased lungs like so many I would fear the cold, but I'm certain I don't. I have had real bad rheumatism in my chest, but I am sure it won't hurt me to come home."

He had finally come to the conclusion that Florida was not the place God wanted him to be. It was as if God were saying, "Madison, have you forgotten so soon the white faced sailor with outstretched arms? He is not here but along the dangerous coast of your own home. Return and I will be with you and give you the strength you need."

He arrived home March 5th, 1887. He had endured hardship, loneliness, disappointment, failure, depression and poor health--all without a friend to whom he might turn. Yet, it was these long, weary months that helped make him so effective in his later work. He knew the sailors he served must have similar problems and long for home and dear ones, too. They would need a friend they could trust; one with love and understanding for those in need. This they found in their chaplain because he had been through it all.

Chapter Four

BOSTON MAKES A DISCOVERY

For some time the Boston Seaman's Friend Society[1] had been looking for someone to open a branch on the southeast coast of Massachusetts. Rumors persisted that such a person, Madison Edwards, was already doing that type of work in Woods Hole at his own expense. They decided that if this young man was everything others claimed him to be, they had better interview him. He had literally thrown himself into the work for seamen when his health returned. This was the promise he made and he never went back on a promise.

The first thing he did was to sell his shoe store in order to buy a small steam launch--also christened Helen May. He expanded his field of labor to include--in addition to Woods Hole and Falmouth--Tarpaulin Cove on Naushon Island and Martha's Vineyard. The next move was to find a reading room in each place.

That opportunity came unexpectedly. Malcolm Forbes, a wealthy yachtsman was greatly impressed by the work at Woods Hole, so he offered the use of a room in his farmhouse on Naushon Island. This reading room soon became popular with the many seamen who anchored in that harbor. Interested people came from New York, Boston and various sea coast cities to observe the new project. They were surprised to find a well furnished room, complete with a new organ, donated by Mr. Forbes, and many things necessary for the sailor's well being. Perhaps that which impressed them most was to see a room intended to seat fifty to seventy-five, filled to overflowing with twice that number. Among the visitors was Miss Esther L. Fiske, of Boston. She returned home with glowing reports which greatly delighted the Boston Society. So in the fall of 1888, three officers from that organization travelled to Woods Hole to interview him.

He was not at home so they awaited his return. Eventually a man with a pail of recently dug clams came sauntering toward them. None of these had ever met him, and the person approaching could have been any townsman. He certainly didn't look like missionary material. As he drew closer one of the group asked, "Are you Madison Edwards?" He acknowledged that he was, and they in turn identified themselves.

"It looks as though you are about to make a clam chowder," one of them said. He replied that he was and asked them to stay for dinner. However, there were chores to be done first. The clams had to be shucked and the potatoes peeled.

"You can pitch in if you want," said the captain. So the three well dressed men carefully squatted beside him and began peeling potatoes and shucking clams.

As they ate they had ample opportunity to appraise their man. They came to the conclusion that anyone who could make the kind of clam chowder they were enjoying, could do most anything. He was hired with headquarters to be at Woods Hole. It was not until March 1889, however, that he was officially appointed superintendent of the Mission, and it became a branch of the Boston Seaman's Friend Society.

The winter of 1888, his first winter with the Boston Seaman's Friend Society was a test of his faith and ability. November was an especially stormy month. The climax came on the 25th, when the winds and waves were so high that the newspapers reported the entire coast of New England was strewn with wrecks. The life saving crews of Cape Cod were kept so busy that many dropped from exhaustion in their rescue attempts. The northeast winds were bitter and many perished from cold while lashed to the rigging. One first officer, safe in the rigging, seeing his captain unable to climb, slid down, stood by his side and was washed overboard with him.

Madison had his share of shipwrecked men in his small reading room, but his thoughts were further over on the Cape. For many days preceeding that storm, he had been aboard the vessels holding religious services. Most of the month had been so severe that he pleaded more earnestly than usual that they accept Christ as their Pilot. Some did, but most didn't. Now they were no longer in the harbor, but somewhere along the coast, no doubt fighting for their lives. How many of those who refused to accept Christ, he wondered, were among the bodies scattered along the shore between Woods Hole and Canada? Reports kept coming of rockets seen or cannon heard from ships in dire distress. No matter how they tried, the weary life savers and the few revenue cutters could never answer all the distress signals. The only thing Madison could do was wait and pray, and later scan the newspapers in search of familiar names.

He was especially stirred the following week by a sermon preached by Rev. Haynes, pastor of Tremont Temple, Boston. The thoughts conveyed in that sermon were identical with his as he pleaded with the seamen of Woods Hole to yield their lives to Christ before a greater storm should sweep the coast. A few short paragraphs of that message follows and indicates the type of appeal made to sailors in that day.

"Do I speak to some sailor whom I shall never see again? Do you take ship tomorrow, boy? Take Jesus with you in the ship. Captain, have a little place for Jesus in the cabin. He will go anyway. Jesus sails in every vessel that goes out of this port. But will you know Him? Will you have Him to help you? Do you want Him to navigate the ship with you? Do you want Him to pick out the course—to peer through the fog with you?

"Hear the preacher plead with you, sailor boy. Take Jesus, take Jesus. He will help you scrape the decks; He will climb ratlins with you; He will toil with you as you reef; aye, toil and tug, and furl and keep your footing upon the rope safe.

He will be with you as you heave cargo, as you almost suffocate down in the stoker's pit passing the coal. He will be with you all the way."

In May 1890, the Edwards' last baby was born, a boy they named Madison Howard. Those early years were adventurous ones in which he learned the ways of the sea as quickly as his father. As he grew older he helped in the reading room and still later, served as engineer of the Helen May.[2]

It was not long before the steam launch, which had been purchased with profits from the sale of the shoe store, became unfit for service. He had still maintained his stevedore job at Woods Hole, and the proceeds from that and his meager salary helped him support his family and buy extras for his reading rooms, but it left nothing to apply toward the purchase of a new launch.

In 1892 he wrote Boston, "I have done some mission work with a sailboat, but it is very uncomfortable this cold weather...When it is very rough I have nothing to protect me." Later he wrote, "I have to walk from the east end of Nauson Island in order to reach Tarpaulin Cove." This was a walk of more than five miles and often made in inclement and boisterous weather. Nevertheless there was an inner satisfaction that came when he drew nearer the cove and saw the many ships at anchor. He later wrote, "I went into the forecastle of each vessel and had rich blessing with the boys. I seem to get nearer to them there, and they open their hearts to me and express their feeling. I am just longing to do more for them." Then he told of an invitation he gave to accept Christ, to a crew of forty aboard a vessel anchored nearby. "To my surprise all but one or two were on their feet, and nearly every one joined audibly in prayer."[3]

He had appealed to Boston for a new launch, but they had their own financial problems. Eventually they realized this need must be met, and made a plea in their publication, "The Sea Breeze," for money to purchase such a craft. They suggested that he try to raise as much as he could, also. In time the money was sufficient and a new launch was purchased. Again the name was the same, Helen May. His love for his daughters had not waned.

Helen May, 1892, when work was at Woods Hole

The launching of this new craft from Little Harbor in Woods Hole, caused much excitement. More than two hundred people gathered to see the new boat splendidly decorated with flags and bunting, slip down the ways and into the waters of Vineyard Sound. Miss Mary E. Jenkins, a school teacher, who was of great assistance to him in his work, presented a class of girls dressed in white, who gave recitations and sang several songs. They were accompanied by a concert organ operated with a crank. Seven and nine year old Helen and May threw a large daisy wreath over the bow, repeating together, "I name thee Helen May," followed by the Christian Endeavor mottor, "For Christ and the Church." A prayer of dedication followed, and the new Helen May steamed gracefully into the sound on her first trip afloat. This was a great day for Madison.

[1] For the history of the Boston Seaman's Friend Society see "A Home away from Home," by Dr. Mervin M. Deems. Furbush-Roberts Printing Co., Inc., Bangor Maine.

[2] Howard died in Oak Bluffs, Massachusetts, on July 29, 1974. the last of Madison's family.

[3] The work at Tarpaulin Cove continued even though Madison was unable to make regular trips. Several dedicated people were appointed as missionaries when shipping was at its height. Mrs. Margaret F. Robinson served for a number of years and always sent glowing reports of the work. Mrs. Janet McDonald and Mrs. Clarence King were among the others. Even as late as 1922 she reported that there had been more large schooners in the harbor that year than at any time since she became keeper of the reading room. That, however, was not to last much longer. The number of schooners began to dwindle. Finally in 1934 the reading room was closed and Austin Tower collected the chairs, bookcase, books and other items which belonged to the Society, and brought them to Vineyard Haven for use there.

Chapter Five

THE FLOATING CHRISTIAN ENDEAVOR

Madison had been thinking for some time about the newly organized Christian Endeavor Society that had challenged the imagination and enthusiasm of youth. "Why can't there be a Christian Endeavor Society for the men of the sea?" he reasoned. While this thought was still fresh upon his mind he contacted Miss Antoinette P. Jones[1] in Falmouth, who had recently been made Superintendent of the Christian Endeavor in that area.

She was so intrigued by the thought that she immediately wrote to Rev. Francis E. Clark, who founded the organization, asking if permission would be granted and the necessary changes allowed.

It was, and with the proper changes made, the new society was named the "Floating Christian Endeavor." The first chapter was organized on the Revenue Cutter, Gallatin, at Woods Hole in 1890. Other chapters were soon added, including the Revenue Cutter Dexter and the Fish Commission steamship, Fish Hawk. Two weeks later sixty men of the crews of the Dexter and Gallatin met with him for a service of praise and thanksgiving. On January 6, 1892, the Gallatin was wrecked on Boo Hoo Ledge off Manchester in a blinding snow storm. Fortunately only one man was lost...the carpenter who was knocked overboard by the falling smokestack. Since that tragedy the ledge has been known as the Gallatin Ledge.

The rules of the new organization were strict, and the pledge to be signed was not as easy for seamen as for the sheltered youth of the church. Newspapers and church

Crew of Revenue Cutter, Fish Hawk

magazines carried the story of this new movement, together with frequent reports from these new chapters on shipboard. It wasn't long before the society had spread to over two hundred vessels, including one chapter aboard a Japanese battleship.

Floating Christian Endeavor on Government Ship

One of the most interesting stories of this period was told by the former Miss Jenkins–the school teacher who had her pupils take part in the dedication of the Helen May. She later married the Rev. Edward L. Marsh and in one of her addresses gave this account of her experience with Madison.

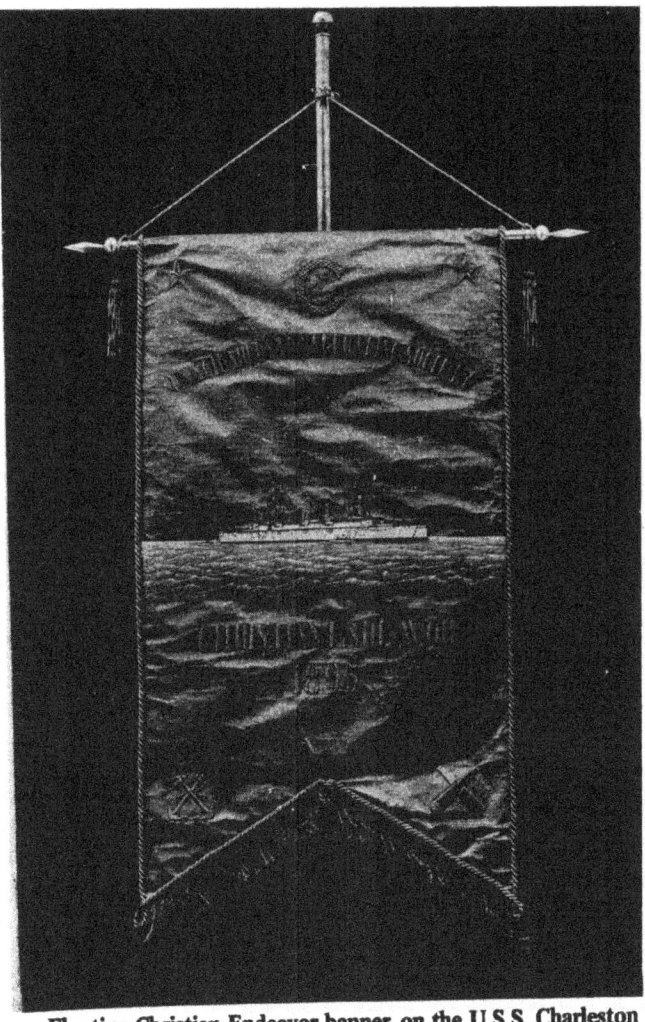

Floating Christian Endeavor banner on the U.S.S. Charleston

"In the course of time I became a school teacher and went to Woods Hole. On my very first Sunday I met a brown eyed man who looked me in the eye and said, 'You are a sea captain's daughter. I want you to help me in the sailor's Bethel.' This was Madison Edwards. I learned to work with him and his sailors. And the work was wonderful and Madison Edwards was wonderful in his work. He learned to remember the names and faces of his sailor friends...He particularly liked me because I had been brought up on board ship and could go up the side of the schooners if they did bob up and down.

Typical Floating Christian Endeavor Member

"We had a large Christian Endeavor Society with a sailor membership. Mr. Edwards gave me the privilege of putting on the pins after the boys had signed the sailor's pledge. One Saturday night a large schooner anchored off Nobska Light. We hoped she would stay there until Sunday afternoon for we were out of Christian Endeavor pins, but were expecting them on every train. They came, and on Sunday morning right in the middle of church service the wind changed. This meant that our schooner would set sail almost immediately. Mr. Edwards did not wait for the minister to finish his fifteenthly--he came down the aisle and whispered, 'Miss Jenkins, the wind has changed and they are making sail out there. Don't you think we could chase them down the sound since we have those pins, go on board, hold our meeting and put on the pins?'

"We both withdrew, boarded the little steam launch, Helen May, and were off. It was an exciting race. We came along side, and thanks to my early training I was soon on board. We held our meeting, pinned on the Christian Endeavor tokens, and bade the boys God's speed.

"Two of those lads never came back. One was badly hurt in shipwreck. He gave his little Testament to his shipmates and said, 'Take it back to Woods Hole and give it to Madison Edwards, and here's my pin--give it to Miss Jenkins.' I think Mr. Edwards still has the little water soaked Testament."

---

[1] Miss Antoinette P. Jones became the World Superintendent of the Floating Christian Endeavor, and was in touch with members of that organiztion wherever they went. With Madison she drew up the rules for that Society. Her funeral was held on Dec. 1918, in Falmouth. The Rev. Mr. Baker who conducted the service, called upon Madison to offer a few remarks, introducing him as the man responsible for starting her upon her life's work for seamen. She worked without compensation, and helped many sailors through the years, especially in the area of education.

Chapter Six

THE ALLURE OF MARTHA'S VINEYARD

Madison had already secured a new reading room in Woods Hole, but his eye was really on Martha's Vineyard. Mrs. Synda Eldridge, president of the local W.C.T.U., graciously permitted him to place two libraries (consisting of twenty-five books each) in their reading room for the use of sailors. The eager chaplain had already inquired about the land upon which to build, and a place to set up a reading room until that building became a reality. He was able to secure from Captain George W. Eldridge, who owned a chandlery at the foot of Grove St., permission to use his loft for a temporary reading room. It was capable of seating one hundred and fifty. He was exuberant.

He hired Mr. Tarvall, a Swedish sailor, to help him in his rapidly expanding work, and his reports to Boston told of the success this man was having with the Swedish sailors. He did not, however, mention the language barrier which often left each other wondering what had been said.

For some time after her visit to the Forbe's farmhouse, Miss Fiske studied Vineyard Haven harbor from her summer home in Falmouth, and came to the conclusion that it would be an ideal spot for a seaman's chapel. She conveyed her thoughts to Madison and expressed a desire to help in his work. This was repeated on several occasions, but Madison, thinking she was referring to the work at Woods Hole, said little. Finally he could contain himself no longer. He wrote, "One winter day she came again, expressing her interest in my work and the men of the sea. This time I told her I would like a reading room on Martha's Vineyard." He concluded with these words, "She said she would build one, and she did." No greater compliment could be paid a great woman than this.[1]

This promise was all the chaplain needed to set him in motion again. He searched in vain for suitable waterfront property. He did, however, discover the possibility of leasing a lot for a term of years. Madison was not discouraged. Instead he continued to figure the cost of the building he had in mind, and sent his findings to Miss Fiske. When Boston heard what had been done, they immediately wrote asking for the figures plus many questions. They were anxious for a place in Vineyard Haven, but they were more anxious about the cost—they had just purchased new headquarters.

In 1893, land was leased and Miss Fiske, by that time, Mrs. Hammond, made good her promise and the new chapel was underway. The building site was in a most strategic spot, at the head of the wharf, but on it stood an old blacksmith shop which must be removed. No other place could have been more favorable, and Madison, who claimed God had called him as "His caretaker of sailors," had an ideal spot for his new undertaking.[2]

In the midst of rejoicing at the prospect of his new building he received an anonymous letter. Excerpts are given here exactly as written.

Vineyard Haven

Mr. Edwards

Dear Sir

I should think you would be ashamed of your self coming over here beging close and money to start a reading room we have to good reading rooms mr stevens[3] and mr long[4] and they are in good shape one at lower village and the other half way and plenty of good reading at both comeing in every day and mr long is a good man and doing the Master will and why cant you tend to your bisness on the other side we have good people on this side to look out for seamen that comes here and we think here that you had better look after you reading room and keep it clean and you will have enough to do without interfering with any other...we think it is a mean pease of bisness and no brotherly love in it...I should think you would be ashamed we dont think that you praid over it much if you had you would not tride to hurt your brother long and brother stephens you had better keep to home on your side and let mr long and mr stephens a lone."

What should he do? He realized a few were unenthused over his many visits, but it never occurred to him that anyone was hostile. He prayed about it and discussed it with his wife.

"Madison," she said, "you have always gotten along with everyone, and you have tried your best to work with others. If God has called them and you, He will find a way to cause everyone to work in harmony, even the unknown letter writer. Rest assured He knows what He is doing." With that the matter was settled.

---

[1] Miss Fiske was born in Niece, France, April 1868. Her father died the same year and was buried there. After coming to America she spent summers at Falmouth, being the granddaughter of James Madison Beebe who summered at Highland Hall in that town. She married Gardiner Greene Hammond, and lived in Boston until she moved her family of six to Santa Barbara, California.

[2] It was not until April 1921, that the Bethel land, leased until then, was purchased at a cost of $3,500.00. A building, the old Oliver store, which stood on the corner behind the Bethel, was sold and moved away, making room for another lawn, flowers and shrubs.

[3] Rev. Daniel Waldo Stevens (the mr stevens referred to in the letter) was sent to Vineyard Haven by the Unitarian Society as a missionary. He established a "Seaman's Refuge and Reading Room" on Union Bluff, a cliff "midway to the head of the harbor." This ministry lasted nearly twenty-five years. Julia Ward Howe spoke at his reading room in the summer of 1873. He died in 1891 after he performed an outstanding service both as a preacher and as a friend of seamen. With his death, the way was opened for the Boston Seaman's Friend Society to establish a reading room. Later the Unitarian Society in Vineyard Haven called their meeting place "Stevens Memorial Chapel."

[4] Mr. Frederick S. Long (mr long) started a "Sailor's Free Reading Room and Bethel," July 25, 1891, near West Chop. He served the needs of seamen well, but had no organizational backing and had to depend on the public to finance his work. In 1894 Mr. Long left the Vineyard and opened a work for seamen in Maine.

Chapter Seven

THE PROMISED LAND AT LAST

The year 1893 came in like a lion. The first three months were so severe that Madison was either ice bound or repairing damages inflicted by it on his boats. A few excerpts from his diary will convey the obstacles he faced.

Jan. 1 Coldest day of the season; bay frozen over; Woods Hole and harbor blocked with ice. Could not get out to boats with mail.

Jan. 28 Breaking ice; repairing damaged sail and dory.

Feb. 6 Ice in harbor; tried to get out but could not. At work on masts.

Feb. 20 The greatest blizzard of the season; snow and gale winds 66 miles an hour. Very cold.

Feb. 25 Cold, floating ice. Went out but got on rocks and damaged rudder wheel.

Mar. 16 Severe west gale. Went to Naushon to take men. Very rough. Stove hole in launch in contact with ice.

Mar. 17 Repairs on launch for damage of yesterday; repaired rigging and masts.

These few references only begin to suggest the hardships endured. In addition to inclement weather he was in poor health that season. He said, "My throat and chest trouble me." The serious illness that sent him to Florida was still very much in evidence.

He was looking forward to the Bethel soon to be built. The one day, June 26, 1893, when he should have been bubbling with joy, he simply wrote in his diary, "Our reading room is commenced today." This sounded less exciting than the severe winter weather.

He had employed Horace T. Tilton as contractor. His first job was to move the old blacksmith shop at the head of Union Wharf, where the new building was to be located. The shop was at least fifty years old at the time.

The Bethel was to be a plain building, 20x30 feet, with a Dutch roof. It would be placed on cedar posts, facing east, with a 12 foot platform across the front. Only one room would be on the ground floor, with space for a well stocked library. The unfinished space upstairs was to be supplied with cots and other comforts for the shipwrecked mariners.

The weather didn't improve much that summer, and many rough trips were made to Vineyard Haven, and the only reference to his new reading room was, "Building progressing." In July he wrote, "Worst storm of the season." August, "Very severe gales, great destruction of shipping, we have been having some terribly heavy storms. My launch went adrift and ashore in one of the gales, but came off uninjured. I went to Vineyard Haven to visit the Marine Hospital. Just as I got there a terrific squall came up. The sound was as white as a sheet. After the squall passed, although very rough I started for home with head wind, tide and sea. I was an hour and a quarter getting over and just as I got in another heavy squall came. Some three or four vessels were disabled by the gale."

It was finished in early October. For many days Madison spent whatever time he could in preparation for the dedication to be held on the 23rd. The new building was put

Bethel after its completion, 1893

in order, and the Helen May fairly sparkled with a new coat of paint. He kept an eye on the weather. The day before the occasion was clear and beautiful and his spirits were high, but the unpredictable weather that had marked the entire year had returned. On the 23rd he wrote, "very stormy."

He visited the U.S. Revenue Cutter Dexter on the 16th, and Captain Jefferson A. Slamm considered it an honor to participate in the dedication. When the officials from Boston arrived, the Dexter was at the U. S. Fish Commission wharf ready to take them to the Vineyard.

In spite of the inclement weather, they received a real Vineyard welcome on their arrival. A committee of women waited at the wharf, and when the Dexter unloaded her passengers, they were prompltly escorted to waiting carriages that conveyed them to the W.C.T.U. rooms where a delicious dinner awaited them.

At 1:30 the ceremonies began. The new building was already crowded and late comers had to find a spot whereever available. Captain Nelson Luce led in the singing of

"Come Thou Almighty King." Because of the enthusiasm of those present, this was perhaps the most stirring singing heard on the Vineyard for some time. It created the proper atmosphere for the Scripture read by Chaplain Nickerson, and the prayer by Rev. S. F. Johnson of the local Methodist Episcopal Church. Mrs. Hammond was in Europe, but a letter from her brother, Rev. George S. Fiske, who also was unable to attend, was read by Barna Snow, and contained this sentence. "May it (the reading room) do great good to the wandering mariners who chance to enter. May the weary find rest. May the sick find relief. May the sad be cheered."

Chapter Eight

THE FURY OF THE STORM

February 7, 1896, two nights before the schooner, Florida, was to sail, Captain Arthur Brown and four of his crew spent a memorable time at the Bethel. The next morning a brisk wind was blowing, but Captain Brown felt it was not sufficient to keep him in port. Madison was concerned, and went to the wharf in time to see the three master, all sails set, heading for sea.

Two days later, their vessel was out of control, wrecked and drifting helplessly towards Salisbury Beach, Massachusetts. She was spotted at 3:00 p.m. as she struck the sand only about two hundreds yards from shore. She could have been miles away as far as reaching her was concerned. It was evident she would soon be smashed to pieces, in fact some of her cargo was already being washed ashore. As the onlookers stood helplessly watching, the crew attempted to launch their yawl, only to have it swept away by a huge wave, soon to come cascading onto the beach as a mass of wreckage. There was nothing left for the crew to do but climb the rigging where they could be seen waving frantically for help. Soon a blinding snow squall hid them from view, and it was evident that in their wet and helpless condition, without immediate help, they would freeze to death. The wind was blowing a gale from the northeast, and the heavy sea was dashing madly over the vessel. The nearest telephone was three miles away, and the first man to spot the wreck, hurried as fast as the storm would permit, and called the police station. They in turn contacted a nearby rescue unit and the life saving station on Plum Island, travel distance from the wreck about fourteen miles by boat and road.

On shore efforts were made to go to the rescue. Several fishermen battled the surf for an hour in a vain attempt to launch a boat. Exhausted, they gave up and waited for a life saving crew to arrive.

The first crew contacted made a desperate march to the site, only to discover that it was impossible to reach the wreck. They then spent their time patrolling the beach. A bonfire was kindled to encourage those on the vessel and a clergyman among the large crowd, forced open the door of an unoccupied house and prepared a hot fire and beds for any who might be rescued.

About 5:30 p.m., after two changes of horses, life saving apparatus arrived at the scene from the Plum Island station. This raised the hope of rescue, but when the line was fired in the direction of the vessel, which now could only dimly be seen, it fell short of the mark. This was repeated many times, but always the wind was too strong for the line to reach the boat. Just before 8:00 p.m., a rocket was fired by someone aboard the stranded ship. Evidently he had left the rigging, and was willing to sacrifice his life for the rest of the crew. It became apparent however, that nothing could be done to answer the signal. Pieces of wreckage lined the shore. Huge timbers were snapped like match sticks and one could only guess what some of the objects once were. A clock with the hands stopped at 6:95 was spotted and retrieved. Shortly before 9:00 p.m. a body was seen and hastily pulled from the surf. It could have been that of the heroic, half frozen man who forced his aching fingers to light a rocket before being forced overboard. An hour later a second body was washed ashore. These first two, like others to follow, were frozen. It was determined that even if a line could have reached the men in the rigging, no one still alive could have secured it. About 10:00 a.m. the masts were seen to fall, carrying all hands with them.

Among the many articles that came ashore was a letter written by John S. Nilson, one of the seaman, to a friend in

Sweden, telling of his life aboard the Florida. He had been ill for some days, and planned to leave the vessel at the end of the present voyage.

Madison fondly remembered their stay at the Bethel. They had been in the harbor many days waiting to cross the shoals. But what he remembered most was that last meeting. Everyone had a merry time during the social hour during which cake and ice cream were served. The crew of the Florida was only a part of the number present that evening, but in view of the tragedy that followed, his mind seemed to rest on these.

On that night he had hoped he might win for the Lord some who had previously been unresponsive to his invitations. His barometer was showing signs of a possible storm, and he wanted these men to yield their lives to their Eternal Pilot before they sailed in the morning. In a simple, direct fashion, which was always his way, he pleaded with them. Among those who responded were three from the Florida crew, but two of the crew brushed him aside with the words, "We'll accept Jesus when we get home." He knew this was only an excuse; he had heard it before, and with an inner pain he did not show, he reminded them that this could be their last chance.

Laughing merrily, they returned to their boat. These were the two whose faces and words haunted the chaplain when the news of the wreck reached him. "God grant," he wrote, "that they found peace as they clung to the rigging that dreadful night, and reached the home where no storms ever come. I shall long remember the faces of those two boys as I talked with them about their soul's salvation."

At 7:00 p.m. the same Sunday evening, while the Florida men were battling to keep alive in the rigging, the three masted schooner, Allianza, went ashore on Plum Island, only a short distance south of Salisbury Beach. The Monday previous this vessel was anchored in Vineyard Haven harbor, where she remained windbound for most of the week. During that time Captain Melanson and his crew frequented the

Bethel and were present at the meeting already described.

After waiting for so long, Captain Melanson decided to leave the safety of the harbor, even though the weather was questionable. Saturday night he was far behind schedule not having yet cleared Cape Cod. Although the sea was rough it was not dangerous until Sunday morning when the already described northeast storm developed. The captain at first turned seaward, but later stood off and set his course for Salem, Massachusetts. The wind blew them much further north, and they landed with driving force on Plum Island.

Because of the excitement further north, and the fury of the storm, she was not immediately detected from shore. She began to break up so rapidly that it was a case of every man for himself almost from the beginning. Captain Melanson, the steward and a young crewman lost their lives. The mate and three others of the seven aboard, came ashore on pieces of wreckage, more dead than alive. They managed to struggle onto the beach and away from the mountainous waves pounding the shore, then lay down nearly frozen and exhausted. Soon one of them saw the light of the Plum Island Hotel and half crawling and walking they eventually reached the building. We will let the manager tell that part of the story.

"I was sitting with two guests in the dining room when we heard an ear splitting scream. It was followed by another and we ran out on the piazza and found four of the wildest looking men I ever saw. We took them in and cared for them, trying to make them comfortable. They were completely exhausted and could not have gone much further." They were given dry clothing and warm food and drink. None of the men knew how they got ashore, but all acknowledged that without the helping hand of God, they would have been drowned.

Seaman Campbell, one of the four who reached safety gave this account of the tragedy.

"All day Sunday the snow and rain were so blinding we could not see and we drifted between the whistling buoy and the breakers. The next we saw breakers ahead. The captain called for all hands on deck and by the time the men were at their stations the vessel struck the sand, but pounded over the shoal and a few minutes later struck about twenty or thirty yards from shore. The waves washed and pounded us mercilessly and the mizzen mast went over the side and was soon followed by the main mast. The fore mast was the last to go and with it went the captain, steward and myself. I do not know what became of them, but think they were tangled in the rigging and are now in the wreckage."

The next day, as in the case of the Florida, the sea gave up her dead, the captain's body having been washed ashore two miles below the wreck.

Chapter Nine

ANOTHER DEDICATION--ANOTHER STORM

It was soon discovered that the newly built Bethel structure was too small. On many occasions the Helen May with a capacity for fifty or sixty men could be seen coming in with over eighty aboard, and towing several boatloads astern. At one time Madison had one hundred and twenty men packed in this inadequate room with more milling around outside. It was evident something had to be done and done quickly. In 1896 the Boston Seaman's Friend Society decided to enlarge it, and have it ready for the next year.

Enlargement was only one part of the project. The plans called for a suite of rooms upstairs for the Edwards family. For sometime after the dedication Madison commuted from his home in Woods Hole, and later the Board furnished one half the rental of a furnished home until the new addition could be completed and furnished.

The work of enlarging the Bethel was done by H. N. Hinckley, contractor, and was started early in 1897. When completed it would be fifty-five feet long, the reading room running almost the entire length of the building, with a rest room and kitchen area in the rear. A spacious fireplace was included, and a porch across the front that could be enclosed for comfort in winter. Six rooms, including three bedrooms were added upstairs, and a piazza overlooking the water, was provided for the enjoyment of the family.

The dedication was held on the evening of October 15, 1897, and again it was accompanied by a storm. The Women's Seaman's Friend Society had furnished seventy-five folding chairs, a new organ, some rugs, curtains and other

Picture of Bethel about 1897. Building at left not yet turned into first fo'castle

necessary items. Interest in the Bethel had grown tremendously since it was built three years before, and once again, though a storm was about to break, no one left. Dr. Dodge of Woods Hole delivered an eloquent address, and Mr. F. P. Shumway, always a popular speaker, held the large audience spellbound with his apt remarks and timely stories. A quartette composed of Mrs. Ottiwell, Mrs. Frank Tilton, Mr. Nelson Luce and Mr. Smith, sang several selections. Miss Mae Norton played the organ. There was also a duet by Mrs. Legg and Mrs. Mayhew.

Mr. Alpine McLean and Mr. Shumway remained on the Island that night, and thus experienced the worst storm in a quarter of a century, as it came screaming out of the northeast. Mr. Shumway very dramatically portrays the scene as he observed it.

"At early morn the head of the harbor near the chapel presented a pitiful sight of many stranded, badly broken schooners, while the shores all about were coated with wreckage, among which the brave townspeople steadily worked, saving here and helping there the men of the sea, to save themselves and the little the gale had spared.

"Higher and higher rose the tide, harder and harder blew

Madison Edwards when he moved his family to the newly built apartment above the Bethel—1897

the gale, thicker and thicker came the snow, until all around was simply a howling, bewildering tempest of frozen sleet blowing seventy-five miles an hour across the angriest, ugliest sea beneath.

"It was then the sturdy, solid wharf began to tear up, and the schooners securely fastened alongside began to chafe, wear and pound until they were crunched and crushed like a baby's cracker. Away goes a topmast, down comes the rigging, off goes the bowsprit like a bit of matchwood, as locked together in a death grip these two schooners wear the life out of each other. A little later the snow cloud lifts a moment, revealing schooners dragging their anchors, drifting toward destruction, catboats blown hither and thither like chips, until the heart of the hardiest veteran sinks as he wonders if the many men on schooners far out at the mouth of the bay are still afloat or have met their death.

"A shout goes up, 'There's another,'" and out into the storm go the hardy men to watch still another schooner now in sight and a moment later absolutely lost to view, as she is driven perfectly helpless towards the fateful shore. 'Where will she strike?' 'Can you see her crew?' 'How can we help them?' are questions asked among many others, only to be answered by a sigh as the absolute helplessness of man is apparent to everyone.

"So the day wears on, and the chapel becomes a refuge for watchers and the watched, who come in to warm freezing fingers and dry soaked clothes. All around is Edwards, stirring up the fires, cheerful and good natured. Even though partly sheltered by the wharf, the Helen May tugs away at her moorings with her windows smashed, pilot house stove in and iced all over."

Thus the Bethel, begun and completed, was ready for whatever work lay before. It had a stormy beginning and anything but a peaceful ending, but no one need apologize for the years of sacrificial service that took place daily in between.

Chapter Ten

TEARS OF SADNESS AND JOY

Many were the letters received from those facing dangers, asking for prayers. For many 1897 was a tense year because of the strained relations between the United States and Spain. The following paragraph from a letter sent by an officer of the U.S.S. Dallas, near the close of that year, is an example. "I hope you have not forgotten the Dallas or us in your prayers, which we need. The outlook is not bright but the future is in God's hand. I know He will give me grace enough to walk the narrow way. Please pray that I may prove faithful. C.B.H."

A short time later he received the news of the loss of many Floating Christian Endeavor members aboard the battleship, Maine. Among them was Carlton Jencks. Carlton was one of the most sincere and active young men in the new movement. To him was due the Christian Endeavor's Seaman's Home in Japan. He was aboard the U.S.S. Charleston at that time and had recruited a large number from the crew for this new religious organization.

Now he was aboard the Maine. She had recently been assigned to protect American lives and property in Havana, Cuba, because of the strained diplomatic relations between the United States and Spain.

On February 15, 1898, the country was horrified by the news that the Maine had been ripped apart by explosives while lying at anchor, killing two hundred and sixty officers, sailors, and marines, among whom was Carlton Jencks.

A short time before the explosion, Carlton led a very earnest prayer meeting, at which time he told of a most vivid

Carleton Jencks (with parasol) with Christian Endeavor group.

dream he had. It concerned the destruction of the ship, whether in battle or by some terrible accident, he was not sure. However, he effectively used that haunting illustration to urge everyone present to be ready for death at any moment. How many of his attentive hearers were lost with the ship we do not know, but at least one escaped for it was he who told the story of the last prayer meeting and the disturbing dream of destruction. We do know that a large number attended and almost all were Floating Christian Endeavor members.

When the story reached Madison, he was deeply moved. "If anyone was fitted for the ministry," he said, "Carlton was that man." No one could adequately measure the good he did, or into how many hearts and homes the world over the Gospel seeds were sown by him. We do know that he helped organize such a religious group aboard at least one Japanese battleship, and many others of various nationalities. The terrible disaster that led to his untimely death, not only brought sorrow to multitudes of adults, but it was recorded that a million Christian Endeavor church youth who had experienced his influence, felt a personal loss.

Madison was honored many times. Although in 1898 he had been in Vineyard Haven only a short time, he had become very popular. August 13 a surprise birthday party was planned by enthusiastic seamen and friends from the village. A short talk was given by Mrs. M. L. Norton who spoke of the "great joy in Heaven over the returning souls due to the effective ministry of their chaplain." Miss Guinn, a very popular soloist of that period, received prolonged applause. After refreshments were served many kind wishes were extended to Madison and his "true yoke-fellow" Mrs. Edwards, with the prayer that their years would be multiplied by God who had already crowned their labors.

On the first of November, 1898, Madison and his engineer, Charles Ericsson, saw the four masted schooner, Alice Clark, of Portland, Maine, with signals set and a large company on board. Running alongside, he discovered that the many people were passengers and crew of a burning vessel that Captain Clark had recently rescued. Madison received them aboard the Helen May and brought them to the Bethel where they were comfortably clothed and fed. Mrs. Hamilton, one of the passengers, after experiencing the rescue and the love and concern shown them at the Bethel, exclaimed, "It's love, love, all love!"

During their stay at the Bethel Madison read the ninety-first Psalm, including the verse, "He that dwelleth in the secret place of the Most High shall abide under the shadow of the Almighty." Although he was unaware of it at the time, 1898 was to be a memorable year for him.

Chapter Eleven

THE PORTLAND STORM

The winter of 1898 and 1899 is still remembered for its terrific gales, loss of a tremendous number of ships and a fearful toll of lives. At the close of those hectic months Madison wrote in his diary: "The past winter has been a very trying one. More shipwrecked men than ever before. On October 22nd shipwrecked men were brought to us and in the great storm of November 26th more than a hundred men partook of our supply of clothing and food. However, over one hundred men asked for prayers and sought the Lord while some went out to do Christian work."

The destruction wrought by the 1898 storm was felt particularly along the southeast coast. It later became generally known as the Portland Storm.

At 6:55 p.m. Saturday, November 26, the steamer Portland on her regular trip to Portland, Maine, left her berth in Boston in spite of warnings from those who had been watching a small storm gradually becoming more dangerous. This storm soon increased in intensity and by the time she reached Cape Ann it had become a hurricane. The last glimpse of the Portland was at 11:45 p.m. when she was struggling and no doubt out of control fourteen miles southeast of Gloucester harbor.

It was fair the morning of the 26th, and even when the sky clouded no one dreamed that hurricane winds would rip the coast that night. Actually the wind didn't pick up until after 6:30 p.m. Chaplain S.S. Nickerson of the Boston Seaman's Friend Society, described the deceptiveness of this vicious storm from his own observation.

"Saturday morning, November 26, 1898, I stood on James Head near Chatham light. Before me stretched the ocean for three thousand miles. The sky was leaden--deep and murky. Not a cat's paw on the water. The sea was calm. Like a tiger it was resting for a plunge that should destroy life. Off on my starboard hand lay the Pollock Rip lightship, surrounded with fifty or sixty sails of vessels, apparently drifting with, or just stemming the tide. Their towering masts and sails stood high in the air. Their white sails mirrored against the black background.

"How little we thought that many of those staunch vessels before twenty-four hours passed, would be wrecked, and the warm hearts that then were beating would lay cold in death, wrapped in seaweed at the bottom of the sea, or lifeless on the shores of Cape Cod."

By 2:00 a.m., November 27, this destructive storm was blowing over Martha's Vineyard. At 5:00 a.m. the full force of the storm, described as a "blizzard of hurricane intensity" was rocking the Bethel and was already destroying the shipping in the harbor. At the Race Point life saving station on Cape Cod the winds were clocked at ninety miles an hour. "Conditions were the worse I have known," keeper Fisher said. It was reported even higher in Vineyard Haven where readings of one hundred miles an hour were recorded.

Every vessel scurried to reach some port. Nearly a hundred turned back to what they considered the safety of Vineyard Haven harbor. Others kept on their northward course. Those returning to the Vineyard reached port late that evening, barely in time for most of the men to get ashore. The snow was blowing so hard that visibility was zero. Many of the late incoming boats were unable to anchor, but anchors made little difference. Large and small vessels were tossed about like toys, as though a giant hand was batting them to and fro, until growing tired, smashed them to bits. That giant hand was especially active in Vineyard Haven harbor. One observer remarked, "No matter in which direction you looked there were masts sticking up everywhere." The Vineyard Gazette added that, "Out of the large fleet of vessels in the harbor, only three rode through the storm uninjured." The larger vessels in the outer harbor swept relentlessly against the smaller boats until all were beached or sent to the bottom. Forty vessels of various sizes were either sunk or otherwise wrecked before the storm ended. When compared to the vast destruction it is amazing that the loss of life was so small.

Wreckage after 1898 storm

The three masted schooner Newburgh crashed into the wharf slicing it in two, almost taking the Bethel with it. It stopped within a short distance of Madison's carefully protected flower garden, but no one was thinking of flower gardens at this time. A few days later Madison wrote, "How can I describe that terrible Saturday night! The gale struck us in its fury about 2:00 a.m. The Bethel reeled to and fro. We were up, and the first thing we saw was the English three masted schooner coming directly for the Bethel. On and on she came, until the wharf was rent in twain and just at that time the soul of the wharf master passed away. Other vessels broke from their moorings. I assisted in launching the first boat that put out to the rescue."

Newburg with bridge build around her bow

The lime ship, E. G. Willard, was set afire and the men aboard had to make a choice between being burned to death or drowning in a roaring sea. Their boat had been blown away so they had no means of escape. Another decision that had to be made was what to do with the cook? He had only one leg and depended on his crutches to get around. They didn't have much time to think, but as it turned out time was not essential. To windward of them lay the schooner J. D. Ingraham. Like the other vessels she was torn from her moorings, and to the horror of those aboard the Willard, she was coming with terrific speed toward them. They watched terrified as the rolling, plunging ship drew near. Then the miracle happened. She struck her target, the force of the blow forcing her to back off, then the wind blew her alongside and remained long enough to allow the men to jump aboard from their burning vessel. Even the cook, still holding his crutches, was able to jump to safety.

The death toll would have been much higher were it not

for the unusual courage of a handful of brave men. Their names are recorded in many places and their heroic deeds will ever live as a sample of the kind of men the Vineyard had always produced. Isaac C. Norton, Alvin H. Cleveland, Frank Golart Jr., Stanley Fisher and F Horton Johnson were the men willing to sacrifice their lives in an attempt to save others. Their first trip, Cleveland and Golart with Norton as captain, went to the schooner Hamilton which was fast breaking up. They rescued five sailors but found they were unable to make the nearer western shore, so they went across the harbor and landed near where the oil tanks are now located. The rescued men were half frozen and were first ministered to at Chadwick's blacksmith shop, and when sufficiently revived, taken to the Marine Hospital.

They had just returned when the Annie A. Booth, a three masted lumber schooner, was seen with decks awash, and six men in the rigging. Johnson, Cleveland and the young assistant surgeon at the Marine Hospital, Sherrod Tabb, as crew with Norton in command, made the hazardous trip to the schooner and returned with the rescued men.

Aboard the Leona M. Thurlow, the crew also took to the rigging. The captain, older than the others, suffered from the cold. The young men wrapped sail cloth about him to keep him from freezing, and together they waited. The snow abated momentarily and watchers on the shore spotted the men in the rigging. The life-saving dory was launched again with Fisher, Johnson and Cleveland serving as crew, and Norton in Command. Because of the difficulty in reaching the other vessels the dory was towed to the windward of the schooner by a tug, and let go. After another harrowing trip they reached the Thurlow, rescued the crew and discovered that Captain Roberts of Bath, Maine, was already dead. One of the crew supported the captain with one hand and held to the rigging with the other until his commander expired. The heroic sailor found his feet and his hand frozen tight to the rope when he was rescued.

The storm was at its height when they returned from the

Thurlow and they were exhausted and half frozen. However, men were yet seen on another vessel and Norton, Cleveland and Golart went out again. Now they had even more opposition. Not only had the storm worsened, but everyone near them sought to keep them from going. Protest, however failed and these three went through the blinding snow and returned with five more men who would have met certain death had they not been rescued.

Schooner Newburg—Madison Edwards, left

Here is how Madison described some of the action.

"Early Sunday morning during occasional lulls of the blinding, drifting snow, we could see men clinging to the rigging of a vessel. Immediately a dory was secured. I furnished her with oars and life lines and then assisted in dragging her to the nearest point to where the vessels lay. After an hour of anxious waiting the dim outline of the returning boat was seen, and in a few minutes the rescued men were in our Bethel. That evening we had a memorable service. Prayers were offered for the brave men who were out in the darkness and storm seeking to rescue the perishing."

While this prayer meeting was still in progress, good news

arrived. Madison continued, "In the midst of our petitions the good news came that more men were saved; then there went up a song of praise and thanksgiving as never before had been heard."

While all ths was taking place in Vineyard Haven, tragedies were sweeping over the entire New England coast. The steamer Portland could no longer buffet the mountainous seas. Gradually she was driven back and further from the shore by the fierce winds.

The Albert L. Butler, a three master, was wrecked near Highland Light, with the loss of part of her crew.

The Pentagoet, a former Civil War gunboat, bound for Bangor, Maine, loaded with Christmas toys and other anxiously awaited merchandise, completely vanished somewhere off the Cape, carrying her fifteen crew members with her.

Five vessels were lost off Gay Head. Nineteen men were rescued by the U.S. life-saving crew, but seven perished.

The crew of the two masted schooner, Island City, were fighting for their lives not far from shore off Oak Bluffs. Their vessel was out of control, and they had lashed themselves to the rigging. She shortly crashed ashore before a group of horried onlookers. The crewmen were too frozen to help themselves, and they watched helplessly as several attempts were made to rescue them. The brave men, whose names are all but forgotten, Fred James and Manuel Chaves, nearly lost their lives in the rescue attempt. Later one man dropped from the rigging and shortly after his body washed ashore. After the storm subsided the other two bodies were taken from the wreck.

At 5:45 a.m. Sunday morning, Keeper O. Fisher of the Race Point Station heard four blasts from a steamer in distress, but because of poor visibility could see nothing. He immediately warned other stations and his own surfmen to be on the alert. At 7:20 p.m. that evening, surfman John Johnson of the same station, spotted something white in the water. It was a life-belt from the steamer Portland. Soon the beach for miles was strewn with wreckage, and bodies were being washed ashore, many with Portland life belts on.

Mingling with the wreckage of the Portland were planks and debris from the coal schooner King Philip. This led to the speculation that she and the Portland collided in the blinding blizzard. As no one lived to tell what happened, much room was left for this theory. None of the one hundred and seventy-six aboard the Portland or the crew of the Philip survived. Only sixty bodies from the steamer were recovered.

Back at the Bethel life was going on at a hectic pace. The Woman's Christian Temperance Union opened their rooms to handle those the Bethel could not accommodate, and many citizens also opened their homes to these homeless men. The Vineyard Gazette reported, "The number of unfortunate men who have sought shelter and clothing this past week cannot be estimated. The Bethel is their headquarters. So much clothing and so many provisions were donated that there was no room to contain it all. Money was also given. The W.C.T.U. gave a dinner on Tuesday, and Vineyard Haven women of the Relief Corps gave dinner for sixty-six men on Wednesday. Enough food was left over for the men's supper on each of these days. Most of the men were later returned to the Society's headquarters in Boston. Only the wrecked vessels remain with us."

Over a hundred men were cared for before they could be forwarded to Boston. The entire length of the reading room was filled with straw, for sleeping. During the day it was replaced with long tables where the men ate their meals. Later they listened to music from a gramophone some thoughtful townsman loaned for their amusement.

The following Sunday afternoon memorial services were held in the Bethel for all the sailors who were buried in a watery grave on those two days. Rev. Alfred Fairbrother conducted the service which was very touching and impressive. The flags were set at half mast and floral decorations were furnished.

After things returned to normal, Madison wrote these

words of appreciation for the newspaper. "I wish to express my sincere gratitude to the people of Vineyard Haven who have so generously and consistently cared for our sailors in the time of the great storm. To those individuals and societies

Shipwrecked men at Bethel after 1898 storm. Notice gramophone, left by citizen for enjoyment of the men.

who contributed money, food or clothing to our needy sailors, to those who gave a helping hand, I wish to say a hearty thank you. I trust the Lord will fulfill His blessed promise to all, 'that it is more blessed to give than to receive.'"

Honor finally came to the heroes of the '98 storm, when they were awarded the Carnegie medals for bravery. Stanley Fisher and Horton Johnson were likewise cited by the Federal Government and given gold medals for their part in these daring rescues.

It was not until a year later, Friday evening, November 24, 1899, at the Baptist Church in Vineyard Haven, that these medals were presented. They received a rousing ovation together with another man who tried to appear inconspicuous. Of him the Vineyard Gazette reported, "The loving friend of sailors and popular missionary of the Seaman's Bethel was the last speaker, and was also another hero of the occasion. He knows the bliss of reward that comes from doing for others. For weeks Mr. Edwards gave himself for the comfort and entertainment of the unfortunate shipwrecked men." Recognition such as this seemed not to have impressed Madison. In his diary he simple stated, "Meeting at Baptist Church tonight. I was invited to be there. Medals given to life savers." He said nothing about his short talk, the inclusion of him among the heroes, or the lavish praise bestowed. He was truly an humble man.

Chapter Twelve

GOD'S ACRE

As a result of the 1898 storm bodies were awaiting burial, and the problem now facing Madison was a proper place for interment. From 1892 until the present he had no choice but to use the Marine Hospital burying ground.

When that institution was established in 1879, they acquired a lot some distance from their building for that purpose. It was probably open land then, but by 1890 it was overgrown with weeds and brush to such an extent that someone described it as being "in the heart of the forest." It contained many graves where a sailor whose name or relatives were unknown, was buried without the presence of a friend and no other accessories than required by law. Reluctantly he had buried his dead there. Now he made a decision.[1]

He wrote the Society of his plan. "November 29th there were four dead sailors in the undertaker's rooms. I have felt there should be a burial ground in connection with our Bethel, and have secured the promise of a lot for this purpose. When obtained, the property will belong to the Boston Seaman's Friend Society. I expect to bury sailors in this lot in two or three days."

A short time later the Vineyard Gazette carried this item: "Funeral services for two of the sailors who perished off Cottage City (Oak Bluffs) in the storm, from the schooner Island City, was held Friday morning. Many seafaring men were present and the service was very impressive. They were then taken to the burial ground just provided by Madison Edwards."

This new lot was described as in "a very pleasant location

on the state road leading to West Tisbury, and will be known as the Seaman's Bethel burial ground." It was evidently secured in haste in order to have a place for the victims of the storm. It apparently never proved to be satisfactory, for some time later a group from Boston headquarters came to see it, helped Madison get it in shape, then went off together, looking for another site. There is no record of their finding any other place, but some months later Madison had the promise of another lot in a privately owned cemetery in Vineyard Haven. All he needed was the purchase price, which he didnt have.

During the rest of that winter things remained at a standstill, but early in 1899, Mrs. Francis J. Ward, one of the vice-presidents of the Boston Woman's Seaman's Friend Society, came to the Vineyard to spend the summer. Later she returned to Boston and prevailed upon the Woman's Seaman's Friend Society to provide the $150.00 needed.

On the night of August 13, 1899, before the check was received, a tragic event occured. A young Danish boy, Karl Larsen, who had just passed through a very harrowing experience, fell from aloft and was killed while his vessel was anchored in Vineyard Haven harbor. Madison went out at midnight and brought his body ashore. After hearing from his mates a little of the story given below, Madison remarked, "This boy has suffered so much! I intend to lay him in our new cemetery lot." The next day the money came, and a diary entry states, "Mrs. Ward came over and we bought the lot and put the sailor boy in it." On the 15th he wrote, "We buried our sailor, Karl Larsen, today, and Mrs. Ward attended the service with us. He is the first to be buried in the new Bethel lot," -- God's Acre as it was later called -- and he was only seventeen years old.

This is the story of Karl's short but tragic life. A few years before his death, he left Denmark for London without telling his mother of his intentions. He was headed for America. In London he shipped aboard the schooner "Eliza" which was bound for New York. Three days later they were rammed by another vessel and had to put back to port. While ashore, Karl and a shipmate were attacked by a number of men, sandbagged, mobbed and carried unconscious aboard another schooner. When consciousness returned, they were far out to sea, having been impressed to take the place of part of the crew who had deserted just before sailing.

Landing in New York, still suffering from the brutal assault, he was sick, bewildered and discouraged. Without money, shoes or proper clothing he began a search for his sister who lived in Brooklyn. As he walked over Brooklyn Bridge he realized that he looked like a tramp, so avoided asking for anything, even directions. As he reached the middle of the bridge he began to pray; then the thought came to him, "Olga is a Christian. She will go to the Danish Church. There I will find her." He had to break his silence for he had no idea where the church was.

When he finally reached his destination there came another blow. His sister had moved. The pastor knew only that it was in the country and advised him to try the Danish Ministry for information. After considerable difficulty he reached his sister's home. When she opened the door in answer to his knock she almost shut it again. Yet compassion prevailed, and thinking him a beggar, she asked if she could help him. Lifting his cap he exclaimed, "My sister!" She knew him then but fell in a faint. After she revived, he took her in his arms and said, "Let's praise the Lord together!" They knelt and thanked God for his goodness in bringing them together.

The next day she borrowed money and bought him clothes and shoes. He soon gained his strength and shipped again for three months. On his return he paid back the borrowed money.

He decided to sail again, this time to save enough money to pay his mother's passage to America. He signed on the schooner "Sarah Fell" for two months. He was suddenly overwhelmed with a peculiar, disturbing feeling–something was going to happen either to him or someone he loved. Once aboard ship, however, he was happy and content. Two hours before the fatal accident he wrote a cheerful letter to his sister which she did not receive until after the crushing news of his death reached her.

When the sorrowing sister was told that her brother's death had made it possible to secure a place for Christian burial for other sailor lads, she replied, "I could not tell at first why my dear Father wanted him so soon, but now I know. It was to make a peaceful resting place for others. I know he was ready to go. My Father took only what was his own."

After the purchase of this new lot, Madison made plans to move the three bodies of those whom he had buried after the storm, and place them beside Karl Larsen. In December he spent much time preparing for this sad mission, and when it was accomplished an appropriate graveside service was held. Now the official Bethel cemetery lot in Oak Grove Cemetery contained its first four graves.

The Women's Seaman's Friend Society provided enough money to erect a stone wall around it. The first picture taken showed a well constructed wall, "composed of rocks that had been collected and pieced together in a uniform and pleasing manner." It was built by Madison and his helper, Mr. Lynch, and was finished June 19, 1900. Karl Larsen's grave had a headstone from the beginning, but to insure uniformity and conserve space, polished white stones would be used in the future.

---

[1] In 1975 the Boston Seaman's Friend Society had the Marine Hospital Cemetery cleared of its years of growth, and provided for future upkeep. This cemetery is actually one of the Vineyard's historic spots.

First picture of the Bethel Cemetery showing Karl Larsen's monument

Marine Cemetery before clearing by Boston Seaman's Friend Society

Same view after clearing

A few of the head boards still standing in the Marine Hospital Cemetery before clearing

Same area after clearing

Chapter Thirteen

A COLORFUL PARADE OF HELPERS

In his early years with the Society, Madison was considerably handicapped by lack of help. In his report for the spring of 1890, he made the request three times for a helper. The third request indicated how urgent it was. Permission eventually came but they cautioned, "Get one as cheaply as you can." He followed their advice and some of them were far from capable.

His first helper has already been mentioned. Mr. Tarvall, who loved the Lord, but was unable to communicate effectively with the English speaking sailor. The next was a sailor who gave his life to Christ under Madisons's ministry, and wanted to be active in some form of Christian service. He volunteered to work without pay while his money lasted, but when his pockets were empty he would go back to sea until he could save enough to volunteer again. One glance at this arrangement would indicate how unsatisfactory it was.

In 1891 he secured one whom he called a "sailor who knew sailors." We know him only as Charlie. "He is just the person I need. Being a sailor, his help in running the launch is a great relief." However, the wages were too small, or the lure of the sea too great, for a year later the report was, "he left me to go on the lightship."

He next reported, "I now have a young sailor who has been in the hospital with a broken leg." This young man didn't appear to be a very likely person for a job that required a strong, active body. How long he stayed or how effective he was, we do not know. In January 1893, after speaking of the stormy weather, he added, "I have had to do all this work alone."

March, 1894, he was asking for another helper. Again he was promised one, and although this man didn't have a broken leg, he was broken in health. Madison received a card from Boston stating, "He is very weak and will need to be very careful at first." He would not even leave Boston if the weather was stormy, but would wait for a pleasant day. This was a rather poor assistant for a chaplain who defied the storms, and needed all the help he could get, especially in stormy weather.

The report of the Society for June 1894 said, "The work has proved to be more exacting than one man could meet alone and Mr. Edwards now has the help of Mr. James on his launch and in the meetings. This summer he will also be assisted by Mr. Roper, formerly one of our workers in Boston, but now a student at Oberlin, Ohio." Mr. James proved to be a healthy and effective worker, and it was with his help that the beach was graded in front of the reading room at Vineyard Haven, and the bulkhead built to keep out the tide.

Mr. Roper was a very dedicated young man. He had been a sailor for some years, and later a worker at the Boston Seaman's Friend Society. For the past three years he had been preparing for the ministry. The summer of 1894 he was in New England, not only to work for Madison Edwards, but also to marry Miss Janet Lord, a greatly loved missionary at the Boston Seaman's Friend Society. They were married August 1st, which left both Madison and the Society without valued helpers.

During the early part of 1895, the Bethel chaplain, while visiting the vessels in the harbor, found the Danish engineer on one of the ships, very seriously ill. He took him to his own home where he received the same loving care that would be given his own son. When he recuperated, he stayed on as a helper and a much needed assistant aboard the Helen May. He was not only a good engineer, but a deeply spiritual man, and he could be seen, almost daily kneeling in prayer with a seaman who had a spiritual need or moral problem.

Unfortunately, it seems, that at this period of Madison's work, the good things were often fleeting. It was not long before this young man's health began to fail again, and it seemed to be even more serious than before. Again the chaplain and his wife watched over him, and eventually he recovered. However, his health was never good, so he decided to leave for another climate.

He had one helper that endeared Himself to the Vineyard people. The Vineyard Gazette called Engineer Charles Ericsson, "a brother dearly beloved in the work of the Lord, assistant of Mr. Edwards in the mission among the sailors." In 1898 he left to go to Philadelphia.

I speak of only one other, a helper he had in 1899. He worked out well for awhile, then a vessel came bringing some former drinking companions. This helper not only became drunk, but boisterously so. In fact, drink made him beligerent. No one can imagine how deeply hurt Madison was, or how hard he tried to help him over this serious situation. He did both his and his helper's work, and that first night remained up with him until morning. The next day "he was off again on a lark with the same parties." The following day Madison wrote, "I feel dragged out. C--discharged. He acts strangely. At noon he cursed me, for I know not what. Kept watch over him all night." The next day, still weary from lack of sleep, his diary reads, "C--went today and I feel relieved."

In between these, he had some good men, sailors who were strong and healthy, but they were not the ones to carry on the work. Not long after in the spring of 1899, a young man was preparing to leave aboard ship on a routine run from New Brunswick. When his vessel anchored in Vineyard Haven harbor, he visited the Bethel as he had done several times before. He was a devout youth from a religious home and the influence of Madison Edwards was all he needed to encourage him to dedicate his life to Christ and the interest of sailors. The result was that a year later, in 1900, Austin Tower came to work, not as an assistant, but like the others before him, only a helper. A portion of this book will deal primarily with this modest man who rose from an obscure position to become, in time, an assistant, and later, a much honored and beloved chaplain.

Chapter Fourteen

THE TURN OF THE CENTURY

Madison Edwards would be out of place among merry-makers. The only celebration he knew came usually as surprise parties or celebrations given in his honor by the Boston Seaman's Friend Society or Vineyard friends.

Take for example his observance of the coming of the new century. Social gatherings were held in places great and small. Many were content to invite in a few friends and have a quiet evening, singing and generally enjoying themselves. Others attended special church services. It was one of the most optimistic New Years ever remembered. Newspapers and national leaders were saying that no previous century had been ushered in with more promise. Everyone looked forward to a full dinner pail in the months ahead. But Madison--how excited was he?

In his diary for December 31, 1899 he wrote: "Went in the harbor in the morning and returned in the afternoon. In the evening we had a good meeting with one expressing a desire to be a Christian'" This was all the celebration he needed--one more soul saved. He and Ella attended a church service later, and on their return were met by a "Christian friend" who offered to help him over the holiday. His notation for January 1, 1900 was simply: "At work at the Bethel all day varnishing and cleaning. In the evening his helper conducted a meeting for the twenty-five sailors and the twelve entertainers present, while he kept a speaking engagement elsewhere.

It was the end of the next year that appealed to him most. In fact, he seemed to consider that, as many did, the end of the century. He wrote on December 31, 1900: "Went down harbor and invited men to the meeting. We had a wonderful time. Fifty men took my hand and pledged themselves to follow Jesus. A sight that I never met before in my experience. We held until 11 o'clock. This evening I never will forget. God grant that this may only be the beginning of so many lives for the Lord. The end of the century so crowns my wish I only have to say 'the Lord be praised!' "

September 1, 1900, Madison took a much needed vacation to Jamaica as the guest of the agent of a fruit company steamer, Admiral Simpson. While there he met a young man, Oscar E. Denniston, who was attempting to do a religious work for the sailors. Madison encouraged him to come to the United States where there would be greater opportunities. He did, and later became a missionary in Oak Bluffs, and finally a beloved pastor of Bradley Memorial Church in that town.

Helen May bringing men ashore—1900. Note vessels in harbor

On Madison's return his work continued without interruption, regardless of the weather. During the severe winter that followed his launch rarely remained at the wharf. On one particularly stormy day, a captain, snug in his cabin, said, "Edwards won't be out tonight." These words were hardly spoken when the quick put, put, put of the Helen May was heard. The captain shook his head in disbelief, and said, "Well, well, this man must be getting big pay for his work, or he is mighty loyal to sailors!"

The next few years brought a pleasant surprise and a dark valley. On August 13, 1902 he celebrated his fiftieth birthday. It was called his jubilee birthday, and his friends planned a party fitting the occasion. Ice cream and cake were served and many gifts received. It was also the tenth anniversary of the founding of the Bethel and the Boston Seaman's Friend Society gave him a fine field glass, a token of their esteem.

On Thanksgiving Day, although in excruciating pain in a finger of his right hand, Madison made his usual trip down harbor to invite men to his evening service. On his return his condition required immediate attention. By evening he became alarmingly ill with blood poisoning. A local physical spent most of the night with him. The next day he was taken to the Marine Hospital, where the finger was removed. For several days his life hung in the balance with chances of recovery one hundred to one against him. For weeks there was great anxiety and a brave fight for life followed. There was much concern throughout the island, and every church had prayer for him. Individual groups met and prayed far into the night. The Vineyard Gazette reported that day by day people waited for the latest news. "Certainly if human love and sympathy can bring health and comfort to this beloved family," it reported, "this Christian worker would be restored to his chosen vocation. They may be assured that not only the hearts and prayers of the floating population in our harbor are with them, but also the village population is united in tenderest sympathy and prayer."

Two days before Christmas he had so recovered strength that he crept down the Bethel stairs from his bedroom to conduct a service for the men he loved. In a letter to Mr. Shumway, chairman of the Executive Committee of the Boston Seaman's Friend Society, he wrote of his gratitude to the townspeople for their kindness and sympathy, and also thanked God that his life was spared. "My hope," he concluded, "is that I shall be better fitted for my work because of the pain and sickness I have passed through."

During the summer of 1903, the Helen May was cut in two and lengthened to forty-two feet, enabling her to accommodate seventy to eighty men each trip. A second and most impressive dedication took place on Sept. 3, 1903. The Bethel was filled to capacity with many standing outside. A piano solo, "Nearer my God to Thee," was played by Mrs. Shugrue; and a song, "Thy Will be Done," with piano and violin accompaniment, given by Mrs. Cordelia Luce.

Madison asked that "Nearer my God to Thee" be sung again as the boat was being launched. He was near tears as he said, "Nothing but that hymn, played and sung by my daughter (Helen) would ease the pain and quiet the nerves during my terrible illness of less than a year agao."

About this time a ten ton smack anchored for a week in Vineyard Haven harbor with only a sixteen year old boy aboard. After the chaplain had visited him, and invited him to the Bethel he knew something was amiss, and became quite concerned. On the night of this boys visit in the Bethel, Rev. Oscar Denniston was the speaker and his text was, "Be sure your sins will find you out." The lad was greatly stirred. He had stolen the vessel and after the meeting decided to take it back to her owners and face the consequences. Arriving in Boston after nearly losing both the boat and his life, he was turned over to the harbor police, tried and sent to Concord Reformatory. When Madison later visited him the boy proudly took from his pocket the Gospel of John given him that night at the Bethel, and reminded the chaplain that he was reading it faithfully. Madison kept writing encouraging letters and the boys answers can be summed up in this one sentence, "I cannot describe the feeling of gratitude I have for you." He later left the reformatory a completely changed young man.

This paragraph is from one of the many letters received

during this period. "I will never forget how you took a sick seaman into your home and nursed him to health. And several years later when a worse sickness came upon him, how those same kind hands and faces tenderly watched over him. Neither shall I forget the family worship when someone read the 91st Psalm, claiming the promise of God that 'no harm shall come near this dwelling,' and how safe and secure I felt after that." H.A.

Chapter Fifteen

A SECOND MISSIONARY EMERGES

Two events of importance happened at the turn of the century. January 23, 1900, the steamer Ardandhu of Glasgow, was run down and sunk in Vineyard Sound. The disaster was so sudden that two members of the crew perished. Twenty-nine others were saved and brought in to the Bethel. They were unable to save any of their belongings, many were only partially clothed when rescued. Chaplain Edwards immediately contacted the townspeople, and clothing and shoes were cheerfully provided. Straw was secured for the Bethel floor and that night twenty were made comfortable and warm. Extra cots were put in the fo'castle for the officers. The next afternoon they left for New York, and while still standing on the pier, gave three cheers of appreciation for the chaplain and the Bethel for the care given them.

The second event was when Madison engaged Austin Tower to be his helper. Chaplain Edwards had little idea of what he was getting when he made that choice. He simply judged this new candidate on his knowledge of the sea, his youth, his desire to serve seamen, his religious background, and the fact that he neither smoked nor drank. This he expected from all his previous helpers, but for one reason or another this dream often faded. Austin Tower was of a different breed, one who was destined to be a successful chaplain himself.

In 1896, when only sixteen years old, he became a foremast hand on a windjamming coaster. His schooner discharged cargo in various ports from New Brunswick, his home, to Galveston, Texas. On the voyage south and again on returning, his vessel often stopped in Vineyard Haven and many of the crew spent considerable time at the Bethel. Madison liked this modest youth and often talked with him about dedicating his life to some form of Christian work.

Austin Tower was born in Sackville, New Brunswick, April 16, 1880. He attended a one room school, but his interest was not as much in his studies as in the exciting tales of the sea told by the many seafaring men of that area, among them many friends and relatives. When he reached sixteen he felt the time had come for him to embark on, what he thought then, to be his life's work. Life aboard ship was not easy, but like many reared along the coast, it came natural to him.

It so happened that on August 13, 1899, Austin was at the Bethel. This was Madison's birthday, and each year on this occasion he held a special meeting, pleading for the men to yield their lives to Christ. Austin was one of three men who responded and dedicated their lives anew to Jesus. After the

Austin Tower when he came to work at the Bethel-1900

service Madison reminded him of their past conversations and asked the question that had been on his mind for some time, "Would you be willing to come and work for me?" His answer was in the affirmative, but he had signed on for another round trip, so it was some months before he would be able to accept. When his vessel later returned to New Brunswick laden with coal, he was paid off and discharged. He then made the long trip by train to Boston, and from there to Woods Hole. Madison met him with the Bethel launch, July 24, 1900.

Although he was hired as a helper, Madison had no idea of his amazing ability. He was a wiry fellow, strong, alert and conscientious. A daily inspection of the Bethel revealed that as a janitor he was as neat as any housewife. As a mechanic he was equal to many trained for that trade. The buildings began to glow as he painted. Madison was a sloppy painter and whenever Austin saw him with a paint brush and can of red copper paint, his favorite, he would quietly step in and taking the brush and can, say he had ample time for the job. Madison liked gardens, and plants and shrubs grew in abundance, but when his new helper proved to be an experienced gardner, he soon relinquished much of this work to him.

Austin Tower 3rd left, front row; Nelson Luce 5th from left; Madison Edwards 2nd from left, back row

With his ingenuity there were few things he couldn't fix. His offered assistance was accepted by many, and children brought broken boats and toys to him for mending.

He cut hair, shaved those physically unable to care for themselves, and gave first aid to many who came to his door. He was adept at repairing boats and motors, and numerous captains sought his help. He was an excellent carpenter. Many times he shingled the buildings, and most of the doors and cabinets were made by him. Many were the times he sat in a bo's'n's chair atop the flagpole, scraping and painting. He had the ability most men would give much to possess, yet he never spoke of these things unless it was drawn from him.

That which perhaps pleased Madison the most, was his ability as a soul-winner. Most reports gave the chaplain credit for the many conversions at the Bethel, and he certainly deserved the credit given. However, Austin, in his own quiet way, influenced more men in his fifty-seven years of service, than any report would convey.

The Vineyard Gazette says of him, "After he gathered the men he would stand before them in role of an evangelist, prophet and counselor. He would lead the singing, give a very earnest, down to earth talk, then seek as many new commitments to Christ as he could. His heart and soul was in his work. He at once constitutes a clergyman, a sea going ambulance driver, harbor master, life guard, and a genuine friend in need to all who venture upon the water."

His spiritual influence was apparent from the beginning. In 1901 he received a letter from a sailor stating that he had never attended such meetings in all his life as those held at the Bethel. Then added, "We had a perilous voyage after leaving Vineyard Haven. The waves were mountainous and swept the vessel from stem to stern. I was washed half the length of the deck, but fortunately was saved. During my peril I thought of the last words spoken at the Bethel, that we should be prepared for whatever danger might await us. Thanks to you and Chaplain Edwards, who made God so real to me, I was able to face this storm without fear." J.B.

Chapter Sixteen

COMFORTS FOR THE SAILOR

"In time of peace prepare for war. Now is a good time in the lull of summer to prepare a supply of comfort bags, mufflers, arctic caps, mitten,s etc. for winter use. There is an unlimited demand for these things, and the winter will quickly come when they will be in great demand." This is an appeal from the "Sea Breeze" for July 1899.

The comfort bag orignated in Boston on a cold stormy April morning in 1872. Seated in a cheery library near the corner of Somerset and Beacon Sts., were Mrs. Silas Pierce, hostess, Miss M. A. Fullmore and Captain S. S. Nickerson, later the beloved chaplain of the Boston Seaman's Friend Society. They met to discuss how to provide the seamen with such essentials as needles, thread, bandages, etc., and how these necessities could be conveniently carried by the recipient. Miss Fullmore suggested, "Why not a cotton bag?" Captain Nickerson agreed, and Mrs. Pierce immediately said, "We'll call them sailor's comfort bags." That very morning the first comfort, or ditty, bag was made.

Later the contents came to include: a pocket Testament which carried a letter from the donor, with her name and address, court plaster, old linen and bandages for injuries, cotton thread, white and black suitable for common sewing and sewing on buttons, thimble, wax, assorted needles, darners, darning yarn, pieces of woolen for patching and as many more useful articles as the bag would hold. A few differed in some ways depending upon the mood and resources of the donor.

Not only were the ladies to make comfort bags, but some

knitted goods also. These included socks, caps, mufflers, mittens and wristers.

Directions for making these bags were issued by the Society. "These are made of bright colored material such as cretonne, chintz, gingham, etc., with a double draw string in the top. The large size for knitted articles should be 12 to 14 inches square, and the small size for first aid and sewing kits, 7 to 8 inches square."

For socks, "Use heavy, dark colored wool on four Red Cross needles No. 1 (diameter one eighth inch). One pair socks uses about one quarter pound of wool. Make the feet 10 to 12 inches in length."

Mufflers: "Cast fifty stitches of dark five-ply Scotch wool or similar heavy dark wool, on a No. 7 needle. Knit plain for length of 1¼ yards."

Wristers: "Make these of gray Scotch wool and use two No. 12 steel needles. Cast on sixty stitches, knit two and purl two for 12 inches. Bind off loosely so the hand can slip through easily. Sew up, leaving an opening 1½ inches from either end for a thumbhole. In this way the wristers can be reversed and will wear much longer."

Socks and mufflers need no word of explanation but wristers may. In inclement weather at sea, oil skins rubbing against wrists wet with salt spray become painfully raw and sore. The wrister was to prevent that. On many an occasion a young sailor would come to Chaplain Tower with red, swollen wrists. After applying an ointment and bandage, he would present him with a pair of wristers.

These bags were prepared by children and women of all ages, and all were encouraged to enclose a personal letter. The men always looked for these letters, and most of them wrote a letter of appreciation in return. The youngest donor was six years old. Here are extracts from letters placed in the Testaments by children. "Dear friend, I hope you will like this bag. I want to call you my sailor. I shall think about you when the wind blows and it storms. I am six years old and this is my first year at school."

Here are two from nine year olds. "Dear Sailor Friend, How are you? I pity you to be out on the ocean when it storms. Have you been shipwrecked? I hope you will find something in this comfort bag that you will like." The second one read: "Dear Friend, I will write you a letter. I hope you will read my Testament every day. I don't want you to drink any intoxicating liquors. I wnt you to be a good man. I will pray for you."

The following is from a little older girl: "Dear Sailor Friend, I hope you are well and have never been shipwrecked on stormy days and nights. I wonder if you like salt water, I don't. But it would be better for you than rum. I hope you will write me a letter. I am twelve years old. I do not like to write letters but I hope you do."

The sailors loved these letters, usually answered them, and occasionaly sent the donor some little gift upon reaching port. Sailors were unanimous in saying it was the letter they liked most, for it showed that someone ashore was thinking of them, caring and praying for them.

It is interesting to note in this connection that some of the young people organized in small groups with the making of comfort bags their project. Some had such novel names as the "Pine Needles." The "Sailor's Little Helpers," a group of teenager girls, was organized, so fittingly, by the chaplain's daughter, Helen Edwards. These and similar group of adults, as well as church organizations throughout much of New England kept the Bethel well supplied with these comforts for seamen.

A poem written around the turn of the century is the story of a sailor who received such a bag. The first verse follows:

> *He was only a "common sailor,"*
> *Fond of bluster and brag,*
> *When a lady at the sailor's home*
> *Gave him a comfort bag.*
> *He laughed when he looked within it,*

> *Buttons and thimble and thread,*
> *Then hung it on the hook close by*
> *To his bunk that served for a bed.*

The poem then tells how, after sailing he was stricken with a fever, and longed for a friendly hand. Eventually he thought of the comfort bag, and opened it. He discovered a Testament with turned down leaf pointing to the verse, "He came to save the lost." Fumbling among the remaining contents he discovered the ever present letter addressed "To one far from home." The sick man said, "That's me." The result was that the sailor was not only healed physically, but spiritually. The last four lines of the poem read:

> *And so one little comfort bag*
> *Brought helpful strength and peace.*
> *And now, dear girls, with faith renewed,*
> *Our labors shall not cease.*

In April, 1904, the schooner, G. M. Brainard, with all her crew, was lost beneath the frozen waters of Long Island Sound. For some time during the previous December, this vessel lay at anchor in Vineyard Haven, and nearly every evening some of the crew attended the Bethel services. During their stay, comfort bags were distributed and each man on board received many tokens of Christmas love. On the Sunday following, the cook, John Nichols, lay in his bunk reading the New Testament he found in his comfort bag. Beginning with Matthew he read the first two Gospels, and it came to him that these words were written for his benefit. The thought was impressed upon his mind that he ought to become a Christian. He came ashore that evening, and standing before the assembled sailors, told of his determination to lead a Christian life. The next evening he came again to the Bethel to say it was the happiest day he had ever experienced. At the chaplain's suggestion he and several others were to start the new year by keeping a diary of God's mercies. Within a few days the Brainard sailed away never to return. Cut through by heavy ice she sank with all sails set, in Long Island Sound. All were lost, but the few weeks at the Bethel and the contents of a comfort bag had helped change the spiritual course of each one.

This and many other such experiences, caused Madison to write, "I would rather have a thousand comfort bags than the best evangelist you can send me."

Chapter Seventeen

THE DANGERS OF ICE

Tragedies came not only from storms or treacherous pea-soup fogs, but there were times when ice was as dangerous as hurricane winds. Many vessels were ripped by ice and others were icebound in various harbors for long periods. In his notes, Madison often referred to the "ice embargo," that made his trips down harbor impossible.

The winter of 1904-05 was noted for its cold and stormy weather. The ice in Vineyard Haven harbor was thick enough to hold anyone walking from most of the anchored vessels. For an entire week the seamen used this as a bridge between their boats and the Bethel. Every night the reading room was packed. On Sunday, February 21, 1905, because of a slight warming trend, the ice became too soft for safety. Yet they came, regardless. That night as Chaplain Edwards was speaking he became aware that the wind had changed and was blowing from the south. Immediately closing the meeting he warned the men to leave and race for their boats, which they did none too soon. In ten minutes after the warning was given, the ice broke and the boats were dragged toward the sound. The Helen May had been iced in for some time and Madison could do nothing to help the threatened sailors, but all managed to reach their ships safely.

The next winter was no better. Pictures taken that year make one an eyewitness to the daring and ingenuity of seamen. Helen left us a pen picture of the ways and means used in getting ashore. "Each man carried a large stick for safety, usually an oar, and several pulled a sled for ships provisions. After supper we could see the lanterns coming

Men from the vessels walking to the Bethel service with the oars and sled for provisions-1906

from all over the harbor. When the ice became more solid the oars were left behind. Occasionally the men would slip through the cracks into the water, but were not easily frightened, for the next meeting they would be here again.

"The second time that year when the ice came into the harbor, it was not strong enough for the sailors to come ashore, even from the nearest vessels. The men of the boats further out walked to the opposite shore near the pier of the New York Yacht Club, and continued by way of the street to the Bethel. The last afternoon, when men came ashore, they certainly risked a good deal. The morning of the previous day the ice let them through into the cold water. In the afternoon's attempt they found themselves on sort of an island of ice with no way out. There they kept their precarious perch for over an hour before extricating themselves. The following morning they tried again, and by means of long jumps, reached within a few feet of the shore where the cakes were so small they didn't dare walk, so they crawled on hands and knees."

During one of the services the wind breezed to the north. Again the meeting was dismissed and the launch was dodging cakes of ice on its way to the vessels. Conditions became rapidly worse, and the skipper could no longer push aside the floating cakes of ice. This resulted in a disabled propeller which made it almost impossible to prevent the boat from hitting the jagged pieces of ice. He delivered the men, and after several jarring scrapes, reached the wharf. Seeing no evidence of a leak, he tied the boat securely for the night. When he looked out in the morning he was shocked at the scene before him. The Helen May was under water with only the top of the cabin windows showing. Men from the ships tied up at the wharf quickly offered their assistance. The Helen May was raised, hoisted up to the nearest vessel and a ragged hole patched.

Another time as Madison went out to collect his men, he kept near the shore to avoid heavy ice. In being cautious he drew too close and grounded. It was a freezing, wet job he and Austin had before they were able to shove off. This was only the beginning. They had barely continued before their searchlight went out, making it impossible to tell ice from water. Again they were at the mercy of the freezing spray before they could get the light in working order. In the murky darkness without the light, they struck a buoy and disabled the propeller. Repairs could not be made and they would not give up and return home, so a crippled craft crept toward the vessels, taking on men, and in the same disabled condition, returned them later in the evening. But the Helen May had taken almost as much as she could stand, and while returning almost gave out. It looked for a time as though the two chaplains would have to spend a cold and hazardous night in the ice, but by working and trying every trick they knew, they finally coaxed her to the wharf at 11:00 p.m. thanking God for their warm reading room and their escape from a worse disaster. "In these narrow escapes," he humbly confessed "I see the hand of God guiding and preserving me."

In the same year, 1906, the Bethel received men from

another wreck, unrelated to ice. They were six survivors of the three masted schooner, Nellie Floyd. She was caught in a terrific hurricane twenty miles off the Frying Pan Shoal on the Carolina coast. She was battered by the heavy seas and winds until there was no hope of her staying afloat. Rafts were formed from the hatches, and set adrift with two men on one and four on another. Captain Matherson shouted, "Good-bye, boys," and with a wave of his hand went into the cabin, and in a few minutes went down with his ship. For forty-one hours the men on the rafts were tossed about by the storm and drenched with salt spray. Without food and followed by sharks, ships passed almost within hail, until they despaired of rescue. Eventually the steamer, Nacoochee overtook the rafts, launched life boats, and the men were brought through the heavy seas to the safety of the steamer. The steamer continued on her way, stopping temporarily in Vineyard Haven harbor to put the men ashore in the care of the Bethel.

During his ministry, Madison constantly kept in touch with many of "his boys." Here are excerpts from one such correspondence during this year.

"I am rapidly nearly my journey's end...everything I have ever done comes before me, and Moma tells me that if I am sorry God will forgive me. Oh, Mr. Edwards, if I could only see you tonight, to talk with you and have you tell me about God and his goodness and have you pray with me, I would feel so much better."

From the same young sailor six months later: "I had another vomiting spell tonight. I am most crazy because this sickness is wearing my mind out. Oh, Mr. Edwards, if I was only a Christian, I would not care, but oh, I do not half serve my Lord. Pray for me that He will forgive me, for I do not seem half able to pray for myself."

Finally: "F—died on the 17th. He talked about you and said he would love to see you. He talked about dying and about Heaven. Before he went he insisted that we write you as soon as he was gone. He picked out his funeral text and hymns. We know that he has gone to a brighter world than this."–His mother.

Chapter Eighteen

THE HOLD FAST BROTHERHOOD

From his earliest days with the Boston Seaman's Friend Society, Mr. Edwards sought an organization that would unite the men in some form of religious brotherhood in which they would be involved after leaving the Bethel. The result was the Floating Christian Endeavor as already described. This was fine while he was in Woods Hole dealing with government vessels and other large craft where a sizeable Christian Endeavor Society could be formed.

One of the floating Christian Endeavor men

In Vineyard Haven he was dealing with the small vessels, tugs and barges of the coastal trade. A good many of them never had a crew of more than five or six, and often were made up from one or two families. The original society that depended upon a large number for success, was impossible here. Recently he and his assistant had worked on an idea that they thought would work, and now they were anxious to start this new organization on January 1st, 1907.

The name of this brotherhood was to be the Hold Fast, based on a passage from the New Testament, Revelation 3:11, "Hold fast that which thou hast, that no man take thy crown." Following is the pledge which members were asked to sign.

"I will strive with the help of the Lord Jesus Christ to live a pleasing life in His sight, and will exert my influence to win others to Him. I will also extend the right hand of fellowship to those who wear the same badge. At least once a year I will send a written word of testimony to the Bethel meeting."

A member having signed the pledge was presented a pin which he was to wear unless he had failed in keeping his commitment. At the center of the small round pin was a white dove on a blue field (from the design of the Bethel flag) with the words "Hold Fast" inscribed at the top, and Vineyard Haven at the bottom. On the flag was the Society's initials, B.S.F.S.

The Hold Fast pin

The Hold Fast had no president, secretary, or treasurer. One dedicated his life, signed the pledge, wore the emblem and lived thereafter as he had promised. Two hundred became members in the first two months.[1]

It was often said that there was no place but what the sun shines on a Hold Fast badge. If this growth seemed spectacular, one must bear in mind that these figures could have been tripled were it not for the care of the chaplains in receiving members. Everyone wanted a badge, but only after he had spent time with the chaplain in his office for counselling and prayer was he allowed to sign the pledge, and become a member. The confession of faith contained in the pledge also carried with it other unwritten restrictions, which included gambling, swearing, stealing, and the use of alcoholic beverages.

The welcoming service for new members usually came at the close of the meeting. Those who had joined previously formed a circle clasping hands with the new members. The chaplain stood inside the ring and with most impressive counsel and admonitions, welcomed those joining that night. He then pinned the badge on their jackets and clasping their hands warmly, greeted each one. Prayer followed in which he commended them to God. The Lord's prayer repeated by all usually closed the impressive service.

There are dozens of Hold Fast stories, but space will permit but a few. A year after this brotherhood was organized, Robert Smith, a fine young man of twenty-three, became a member. He had never committed his life to Christ, and one evening Madison placed his arm around his shoulder and asked, "Isn't it time you became a Christian?" He replied he thought it was and a pledge card was slipped into his pocket. When two days out, Smith became so eager to commit himself to the Christian life, that he begged a Hold Fast badge from a friendly Canadian shipmate. Arriving at St. Johns he went ashore for a while. On his return, in jumping from the pier to his schooner, he fell overboard, was apparently injured, and drowned. He was the first of the

Hold Fast members to lose his life.

On the 23rd of January, 1909, the Helen May was suddenly called to hurry down harbor with a doctor to the Lehigh Valley Company barge, Boston. There two men were found dead, having for many hours been exposed to the fumes of burning coal. A third man, the captain, showed signs of life, and was hurried ashore to the Marine Hospital, where after many hours of unremitting treatment, he was resuscitated.

Of the two who were dead, one was a member of the Hold Fast, a youth from Plymouth, Massachusetts. Telephone messages were exchanged with his parents. The body was prepared for burial then taken by the chaplain to the boy's home. On behalf of fellow Hold Fast members, a floral wreath bearing the letters "H.F." was laid upon the casket. The body of the other, Charles Hughes, after a service in the Bethel, was tenderly laid away in the sailor's lot in the cemetery.

In April 1911 Madison reported that there had been so many wanting to join the Hold Fast that "I have had to hold them back for want of badges."[2]

Among the letters received about this time, was one from the wife of a Hold Fast Captain lost at sea. She was the mother of eight children. The oldest boys, sixteen and seventeen, wanted permission to join the Hold Fast. She wrote, "It is with a sad heart that I write you a few lines to let you know that my husband was drowned in the wreck of the John Irvin, which foundered off Beaver Harbor...My husband thought a great deal of your Hold Fast pin, and he was wearing it when he drowned. He was a very changed man ever since he joined your society."

---

[1] By 1915 sixteen hundred seamen had enrolled, representing twenty-five nationalities and creeds and by that date the Hold Fast pin could be seen in almost every port in the world. In the years that followed that number doubled. It was not until Madison prepared the way for others to follow, that the Anchor Alliance was formed in the Boston Society.

[2] It has been estimated that three quarters of the Hold Fast members began their

Christian life under the ministry of the chaplains at the Vineyard Haven Bethel. Members are not received any more; the book was closed when Chaplain Tower retired. However, even today, visitors to many of the villages along the eastern seaboard, may find an occasional member still wearing that badge of honor.

Chapter Nineteen

STORY OF THE ARANSAS

The steamer Aransas, owned by the Joy Line of Providence, Rhode Island, was rammed by a clumsy barge off Pollock Rip in 1905. She went down in fifteen minutes. Fifty of the passengers and crew were brought to Vineyard Haven. It was midnight and every place where they could possibly stay had long been closed. They were a homeless, cold and forlorn group without anyone to welcome them. The captain of the tug that brought them, knew where to go. There were no lights in the Bethel, but he was sure that in answer to his knock, the lights would come on and the doors would be opened, and his shivering charges given a warm welcome.

The chaplain and his wife were soon on the job. While she and her daughters started preparing food and coffee, he was getting the fire up and preparing places to eat and sleep. Within a few minutes Austin arrived, and between them soon had everyone as comfortable as their limited space would permit. They had some problems. A few were sick from the recent ordeal, and were given special attention. Among the rescued was a captain's wife about to become a mother. This caused some concern, but when they discovered that she lived up to the reputation of being a hardy seaman's wife, they continued to minister to the crying children, and those weak and exhausted. By now the townspeople who had been alerted to the tragedy, began arriving with food, clothing, and helping hands. All night this tender ministry continued, and when morning came the occupants of the Bethel were tired but happy.

As a result of the care given the unfortunate victims that

night, the Joy Line presented to the Bethel their life boat No. 4, which was appropriately named, Aransas, and a small engine installed. The forward section was closed in on three sides, providing shelter enough to be used for much of the lighter work of the Bethel. In 1909 the small engine was replaced by a ten horsepower motor.

Aransas, Austin Tower, Madison Edwards

As the Aransas cost less to run and could be handled by one man, she was often used for ferrying men to and from the shore, weather permitting. On one occasion rough weather proved almost too much for her as Chaplain Edwards relates.

"We had quite a large fleet in. Austin was sick and Howard (Edwards) was spending the evening with friends up Island, so I thought I would try to pick up the men alone in the small launch, Aransas. I started alright, but when I got well down harbor, the wind blew up so it was getting very rough. I took aboard about eighteen men. Others were giving signals, but I got a little afraid of the gale and pulled for the pier with what I had.

"After a fine little service I put out to return the men to their ships. When we got well out to the sound where the seas were rough, and with two vessels still far to windward of us, the shaft slipped and the disabled boat drifted. We tried to work out under sail, but it blew so we couldn't carry sail, and we came back with a fair wind, to the Bethel, intending when Howard came back, to go out in the big launch, Helen May. It was a long wait of nearly three hours, for an accident delayed the motor car in which he came.

"Meanwhile we put on the coffee pot, got up a lunch, gathered round the table and had a merry time.

"It was blowing hard when we finally took the boys out to their vessels, and it was half past one in the morning before we got back to our moorings. All the boys said they would never forget the pleasure of the occasion, and one who took a stand for Christ that evening said it was the night of all nights for him."

On one occasion in 1910, the Aransas was stolen from the wharf, and was missing for several days. An intense search was made along the coast. It was finally found at Harwichport, Massachusetts, by Howard Edwards. The culprit was a boy of seventeen.

Chapter Twenty

THE BETHEL EXPANDS

Madison now turned his thoughts to an adequate building to house shipwrecked sailors. While he was in Woods Hole, shipwrecked, sick, and injured seamen were cared for in his own home or the home of neighbors. However, when the Edwards family moved into the upstairs quarters of the enlarged Bethel, there was no place for these unfortunate men.

First fo'castle at left.

Since there were no available funds for such a project, he turned his attention to two old buildings on the south side of the property that might be put to use. In 1899 Madison decided to turn the larger one into a fo'castle. During a period of weeks, sailors with leisure time, offered to turn their hands to carpentry, and under the direction of experienced townsmen, the building was soon declared satisfactory for its purpose. There were two bedrooms, accommodating four men each, which were in constant use from the beginning. To Madison, however, this was not an ideal situation.

1905—Fo'castle at left unsatisfactory

In 1906 he obtained enough money to erect a cottage type building that was to last as long as the Bethel remained under the jurisdiction of the Boston Seaman's Friend Society. It had dormer windows on one side with a view of the garden, as well as the activity on the wharf.

This new building had two upstairs rooms, one large enough not only for sleeping, but was equipped with stove, dishes and cooking utensils. The first floor was used for a workshop and boathouse. Many were the times it overflowed with shipwreck victims.[1]

Also in 1906 an office was built on to the south side of the Bethel. Previously a corner of the main reading room served this purpose, but accorded him no privacy which he needed for counseling and prayer. This important little room was made possible through the gifts of friends of the Bethel.

Fo'castle built in 1906

The big ships were continually at the mercy of wind and wave, and the chaplain often received letters from the men, telling of the dangerous and frightening experiences they had faced. Following are two excerpts.

Chaplain's first office

Shipping in harbor early 1900.

"We had a nice run from the Vineyard to Chatham on Cape Cod, and then the wind struck in ahead and blew a gale which drove us off shore. There was a heavy sea running with north west gale winds which caused the vessel to labor heavily and spring a leak. This caused us to pump steady seven days and nights at the peril of our lives. A heavy sea continually washed over us and she iced up so bad that we hardly worked her. We expected to sink every minute. The fifth day we sighted Matinieus rock but we couldn't get into any harbor. On the 7th day we were off the north shore of Grand Manan. It took the life saving crew of nine men three days chopping ice and towing us into a place of safety. Our sails were gone, so badly frozen we couldn't do anything with them. My shipmate had his feet, fingers, elbows and hands quite badly frozen. The mate froze his feet, the captain his nose, and I froze my wrist, chin and nose. If we had been outside another night we could have perished. It was through the hand of God alone that we were saved." K.S.

This second letter came in April from a crew member on a vessel in southern waters.

"We left Ponce the 19th of March with half a barrel of

flour, half a barrel of salt meat and one barrel of potatoes. Ten days after Ponce we had nothing to eat but three biscuits full of maggots, a cup of coffee and molasses. Previously a big storm struck us and we only had a double reef foresail. The storm stood for forty-eight hours and we drifted seventy-five miles back. We were exhausted when we came into Mobile. When we had nothing to eat I wasn't scared because I had my trust and hope in God. I remembered the night in the Bethel when I dedicated my life to Him. I kept singing the hymn you had us sing there, 'Ask the Saviour to help you,' etc., and I did so." M.B.

A Unitarian lady visitor in Oak Bluffs had an unusual and interesting experience. She learned that the nearest church of her denomination was in Vineyard Haven, the next town. One Sunday evening she took the trolly to attend a service in that church. The car stopped at its usual place, and everyone got off. She observed many entering a cozy little red building nearby and she followed. The speaker that evening gave a glowing and persuasive talk. "That is a different Unitarian service," she thought. She was also very interested in the man with the moustache who presided. He had such a free and easy style that he held everyone's attention. Another attraction was a large group of sailors who sang as though they meant it. "There must be seventy-five at least," she thought to herself. She left full of enthusiasm. When she arrived home she said to some of her friends, "I've struck the livest Unitarian Church I've ever attended. Everything went with a rush. I couldn't get over the number of young men who were there. And how they could sing! I'm going there again soon." Her listeners were skeptical and asked her to describe the meeting house. They replied with a laugh, and informed her she had attended the Seaman's Bethel.

---

[1]The wheels of progress eventually led to its demise. It was purchased and moved to Edgartown where it is in use as a dwelling, but for those who knew it in an earlier day, it is still full of fond memories, and will remain in their thoughts as a refuge for the men of the sea.

Chapter Twenty-One

WEDDING BELLS, A LIGHTHOUSE AND SOME PROBLEMS

When Austin Tower began his work at the Bethel he stayed at the Mansion House, not far away, but when the fo'castle was built in 1906, a room was reserved for him. Here he lived for two years, until after his marriage when he took his bride to their newly completed home on Mt. Aldworth.

In 1907 he attended Mt. Hermon School at Northfield, Mass. for four months, taking summer courses that would make him a more effective evangelist and leader. While away, his engagement to Helen Edwards, a most faithful assistant to her father, was announced. They were married June 3, 1908, in the Bethel by the Rev. Cyrus P. Osborne, Secretary of the Society in Boston. This was one event that caused rejoicing throughout the Island. Shortly before the wedding, a kitchen shower was given at the home of Ruth Eldridge White, in which girls from her Sunday School class and other local friends participated.

After reporting that the Bethel was decorated with daisies and ferns, Ella gave the following account of the wedding in a letter written her brother.

"Ruth and Nellie came down to help decorate. They stretched a fishnet across the end of the Bethel, over the lockers and to the top of them, bringing it forward in the middle to form a canopy ending with a bunch of snowballs. It was outlined with a daisy chain and fishnet filled in with small branches of oak. Great pails of daisies stood at each end and bunches of daisies were placed around the room. Two large palms and a rubber plant were also strategically located.

**Helen Edwards at the time of her
marriage to Austin Tower — 1908**

"Helen wore a quite plain princess style dress with a small vail with three folds on the bottom. She carried a bouquet of lilies of the valley. Just before the ceremony six girls entered with ribbons of crepe paper, held up with bundles of daisies and took their places on both sides of the aisle. Howard (Edwards) was usher and May (Edwards) was maid of honor.

"As the wedding march, played by Betha Look, began, Rev. Osborne and Austin came in from the entry way. From the front of the Bethel came two little cousins of the bride, one bearing the marriage license and the other the ring, which was placed in the middle of three pinks, tied in one, walking slowly past the girls forming the aisle. They were followed by the bride's sister, May, then Madison with Helen leaning upon his arm. A beautiful and touching service then followed.

"The refreshments were in charge of Walter Norton, who made the strawberry and vanilla ice cream in brick form. Plain and frosted cupcakes and fruit cake were also served.

"As the newly married couple left, a group of young people chased their carriage down the West Chop road, through Tashmoo woods, down by the cemetery and old Edgartown road, to their recently built home. They left after the young couple refused to come out. The next morning they came to the Bethel for breakfast, then left on the 7:00 a.m. boat for a honeymoon trip to New Brunswick."

When the couple arrived home, Austin found he had been promoted to assistant chaplain. His routine tasks remained the same, but Madison had something else in mind, too. He had decided that some lasting monument should be erected in the Bethel cemetery lot. Monuments were in abundance for men who died in our wars, but why not one for the peaceful men of the sea? It was finally decided to erect a lighthouse, but who had the ability to tackle such a project? Austin. With specifications secured from the United States Lighthouse Board, the young man eagerly began the task before him.

Trip after trip the little Helen May made to Naushon and Nashawena Islands, always towing back carefully selected stone which had to be the right shape and size and polished smooth by the sea. It was estimated that thirty-nine tons were transported by the hard working Bethel launch. Soon the stockpile was sufficient to begin the work. During this time the ship captains were busy raising money for the expense that would be involved.

As the work progressed, granite slabs were cut and placed upright to provide support for the top. The cap, cut to finish the tower, weighed a ton. With the help of seamen whose vessels and tugs were in the harbor, a derrick was rigged and it was swung into place. Red glass was fitted between the slabs and a ship weathervane was placed on top.[1] The lighthouse stands twenty-one feet from the ground to the top of the weathervane. It was a most fitting memorial to the men of the sea. It can also be considered an enduring memorial to its builder, Chaplain Austin Tower.

This lighthouse has been praised by many as one of the most unique and impressive monuments built to those who lost their lives in peaceful pursuits. Sometime after its erection, a bronze tablet with the following inscription was placed upon it:

1910
BOSTON SEAMAN'S FRIEND SOCIETY
THIS MONUMENT WAS BUILT
BY CONTRIBUTIONS FROM
COASTWISE SAILORS
IN MEMORY OF SHIPMATES
AT REST

The completed lighthouse in the Bethel lot

These were two pleasurable events, but there were always problems and difficult situations to be met. Occasionally a seaman would accept transportation ashore on the Bethel boat, presumably to attend activities there, but would sneak away to Oak Bluffs where alcoholic beverages were available. Aggravating this problem was the fact that the trolly between the two towns stopped within a few feet from the Bethel. This was all very disturbing to the chaplain, as he promised the captains that he would return his men sober, and on time.

On one of these occasions the chaplain did not realize until time to return the men to their ships that one man was missing, and there was nothing for Madison to do but to go after him. Their conversation on the way back was not recorded, but it must have had a decided effect upon this seaman, for some time later he wrote, "I am trying to be a good boy. I've been drunk only once, but I have sworn off now. I am going to sign the pledge. It gets me in all kinds of trouble. I am awful sorry I didn't attend the Bethel, but I will next time. From your would be Christian friend, J.J.M."

While Austin was attending Mt. Hermon in 1907, he received a letter from Helen in which she wrote, "There has been a fleet here all week, but the crowd of boys did not suit papa. When the service began they would sit in the back seats, and when the service was over they would leave the room. You know papa doesn't enjoy that kind of people." Here, apparently, were sailors who felt they had fulfilled their responsibility by sitting out a service they had no interest in, then instead of enjoying the fellowship, went elsewhere. Men like this were recognized when they came to the Bethel, and every effort was made to win each one to Christ.

Bethel decked out for special occasion—early 1900

Sailors were not the only people who concerned Madison. A new dance hall had opened in Oak Bluffs and this was at the time when dancing was considered a tool of the devil. He wrote, "The boys and girls of Vineyard Haven are going to destruction. The conductor told me that last Saturday evening he had a hard time controlling the young people on the electric car, and they were Vineyard Haven boys and girls. Some were drunk and were very rough. I don't know how Christian people in Cottage City (Oak Bluffs) can agree to continue that evil, or how Vineyard Haven Christians can stand it."

In another letter written by Helen, she spoke of the drunkenness on the part of sailors, many of whom they both knew. These seamen did not enter the Bethel, but were creating a disturbance not far away. She wrote, "What will Vineyard Haven come to? I hope something is going to be

Austin Tower decked out for special occasion — early 1900

done and I believe there is something in the wind to that effect."

She was right. A building near the Bethel was selling liquor to the sailors, and Mr. Shumway and Madison went to the selectmen about the matter. Mr. Shumway was the spokesman, but after he finished the chairman of the Board turned to the chaplain and asked, "Do you ask us to have this place shut up?" "Yes," Madison replied, and the chairman said, "It shall be done."

On one occasion Austin surprised some men gambling in their fo'castle. He watched a minute, then as he turned to leave, said, "Well, boys, you seem to be having a good time." Two of the men were Hold Fast members and they read the hurt and disappointment in his words and expression, and they were ashamed. One covered his face while the other dived under the table. Shortly after, one of the culprits handed a letter to Chaplain Edwards containing his badge and pledge, and a note pleading to begin again. It wasn't long before he was proudly wearing the badge once again. Such a lesson was long to be remembered.

---

[1] It took five years to complete the monument, being finished in 1913.

Chapter Twenty-Two

ALL HANDS ON DECK

Nineteen hundred and nine was both a tragic and happy year. The Helen May was rocked by explosion in the beginning, and a violent storm swept the coast in December with terrific loss of life. In between one of America's noted criminals was converted due to the relentless efforts of Madison during the previous few years.

On a day in February of 1909 just before starting out to pick up the men for the evening service, the Helen May's gas tanks were filled. Unknown to the chaplain, some gas had leaked into the bilge, and as a lampstove was passed from the cabin into the pilot house, a tremendous explosion occurred. The roof of the pilot house was lifted off, all the cabin windows were blown out, and the sound was heard a half mile away.

During her whole history this Bethel boat had been remarkably exempt from accidents. Again these two men were saved from serious injury. Austin, in the engine room, escaped without injury; the chaplain had his clothing torn, his hair, moustache and eyebrows singed, and his right ear burned. Because of his appearance he was hesitant to attend the Bethel meetings, but his daughter, with a piece of charcoal pencilled on a set of eyebrows, and he was soon back on the job.

In the early days of the Bethel, before modern means of communications became available to small vessels, shipwrecks were common. In slightly over a one year period the Bethel suffered the loss of a large number of its most faithful sailor congregations.

In December of 1909, the five masted schooner, Governer Ames, struck on Winkle Shoals off Hatteras and within a short time went to pieces. Repeated attempts were made to launch rafts and boats, all ending in failure. The captain, with help from the crew, lashed his wife first to one place and then another for safety, only to look on in horror as a mast fell, crushing her. Not long after the captain and twelve crewmen perished. The only member saved was Josiah Spearings, who after being tossed overboard, clung to a piece of wreckage through that long, rough night and was picked up the next day bruised, and semi-conscious, by the steamship Shawmut.

Not long afterwards, the five masted schooner, Davis Palmer, Captain LeRoy McKown, left Newport News, Virginia, for Boston. She ran into a fierce blizzard on Christmas eve, and about midnight anchored near what was called the "Graves"--A section of dangerous rocks at the entrance to Boston harbor. Dragging her anchor, she was drawn to Finn's Ledge, and shortly after sank with all hands on board.

Late that afternoon while the vessel was still off Cape Cod, passengers on a Boston bound steamer saw the men gathered in a group on deck and heard them singing Christmas carols. How often those men had sung lustily, the gospel songs at the Bethel meetings, and Madison felt a peace in knowing they were still rejoicing in the Lord through song.

The New Year continued to bring its uninterrupted flow of sad tidings for the Bethel chaplains. Late in January, 1910, the four masted schooner, Henry B. Fiske, was found off Nantucket, bottom side up, apparently a victim of one of the terrific gales sweeping the coast. Madison was deeply touched when he received word there was no sign of life.

At the end of the winter, an article appeared in the Boston Post under the headline, "Furious Winter's Wrecks." In it was the following paragraph, and a list of the shipping disasters of which a few are quoted,

"Never in the memory of living New Englanders have the

'Men who go down to the sea in ships,' paid such a heavy toll to the fury of Neptune as during the current winter. Storm after storm has lashed the coast, storms which even those versed in every branch of seamanship and devoid of all sense of fear could not weather.

"Dec. 16--Four-masted schooner Martha S. Bennett left Jacksonville for New York and has never been heard from since. She carried 10 men.

"Dec. 18--Four-masted schooner Maggie S. Hart left Jacksonville for New York and has never since been heard from.

"Dec. 19--Four-masted schooner Auburn, sailed from Brunswick, Georgia, for Philadelphia, and has not since been heard from. Captain Charles W. Bates and crew of seven men missing.

"Dec. 23--Four-masted schooner Ann R. Bishop left Mayport, Fla., for Elizabethport, N. J., and has not since been heard from. She carried a crew of eight men.

"Jan. 21--Three-masted derelict, believed to be the Edgar C. Foss, which left Charleston, S.C., for New York and never arrived, picked up by the revenue cutter Androscoggin. Captain and seven men lost.

"Feb. 5--U.S.S. Nina with crew of 32 men last seen. After a general search by government vessels from every port on the coast, she is practically given up as lost.

"Feb. 16--Two-masted schooner George E. Prescott, from Rockland, Me., towed into Gloucester by the revenue cutter, Androscoggin. Crew of four men lost.

"Feb. 17--Unknown derelict schooner sighted off Chatham, bottom up, and revenue cutter Acushnet dispatched to tow the same into port. All hands lost."

After spending some days in Vineyard Haven harbor, a fleet of fourteen schooners, two ocean tugs and six barges sailed for eastern ports on December 14. What was called an ocean tornado formed southeast of Nantucket, and the weather bureau failed to detect it, as it whirled up the coast with deadly force, directly at the departing ships. The captains and crews of most of these boats had been coming to the Bethel for years.

The Marcus Edwards and the Mollie Rhodes were two of this fleet, and all hands were lost on both vessels. It was with a heavy heart that Madison sent his reports to the Rev. Cyrus P. Osborne, Corresponding Secretary of the Boston Seaman's Friend Society. I give these reports as written, for they tell a story not found in the newspaper accounts.

"In the great destruction of vessels off the Cape were many of the men we have had at the Bethel for ten days or more. The last meeting, Wednesday evening, was full of interest. More than twenty of these dear fellows said that with God's help they would live Christian lives. It was a most remarkable meeting. It seems like a dream to have so many with me one night, so comfortable and happy, and the next night battling for dear life until death claims many of them."

A second letter was sent a few days later, showing again the profound effect this tragedy had upon him. "Last Wednesday, the night before the great storm we had about fifty men ashore, sailors and captains, and a most wonderful meeting, a great move of the Lord by so many. Captain Dan Dobbins of the Mollie Rhodes, of Vinalhaven, and Captain Webb Robbins, of the Marcus Edwards, Bangor, Maine, were our staunch friends. The loss of these dear men and their crews is a severe blow to our work.

"Some of the escapes were remarkable. Four crews which were here that night were saved by the revenue cutter. We had twenty-five captains with us one night, and the meetings were full of interest no words can express. Since the loss of these men we have had our Bethel filled night after night, and many seeking a new life."

Still later, when the final scraps of news had filtered in he wrote, "The great storm carried down a large number of our dear men that are the light and help of our work. I have learned today that a number of our Hold Fast boys have gone. They were with us the night before. One of them I had in my office where we had a pleasant heart to heart talk and prayer, and the very next night he was in eternity."

Less than a month later, three barges, heavy laden with coal, broke adrift from the ocean tug, Lykens, which was towing them, and drifted within the fatal line of breakers at Peaked Hill Bar. They were the Trevorton, Captain F. A. Brown and six crewmen bound for Portland, Maine; the Corbin, Captain C. M. Smith and four men, headed for Portsmouth, New Hampshire; and the Pine Forest, Captain M. W. Hall and four men, whose destination was Marblehead, Massachusetts.

By morning two of the barges were breaking up under incessant pounding of the heavy seas. Three life saving crews were on the beach at dawn but were powerless to help as it was impossible to launch a life boat, and all other methods were of no avail. The Pine Forest was a half mile away, too far to be reached by a life line. She was enveloped in a seething mass of angry sea, and the men in the rigging were vainly trying to call for help from the shore.

By 9:00 a.m. she was seen breaking up. The men clung to their precarious perch for another hour then made a desperate attempt to launch their own boat. They had hardly taken their places when another tremendous sea smashed against their barge and sweeping around her stern, struck their small boat, hurling the occupants into the seething water. Not one was saved.

These are but a few of the tragedies that occurred during this short span of time. As a result one cannot wonder at the cry of anguish from Madison, when he wrote, "Oh, Mr. Osborne, this has been a hard blow..." At this point words seemed to fail, and he tried to blot from his mind the tragic events of the recent past.

Taking his pen again, he added, "At our recent meetings we have had graphophone records taken of the singing, so when we like we can hear the boys sing. One record on which were recorded, 'Oh, Happy Day,' and 'I Have Anchored my Soul in the Haven of Rest,' were sung by a group of men who were lost when their ships were wrecked the following night off Cape Cod."

Chapter Twenty-Three

THE CARUSO OF THE BOWERY

"Christ came to me in New York, December 13, 1909. I was twenty-nine years old at that time. My hands were black with every crime a man could commit--except crimes against women. Forty-seven times I was imprisoned for offenses ranging from petty larceny to manslaughter. I figured if Christ could do anything with a guy like me, it was up to me to give him a chance.

"On this night I was going to a place in Chinatown called 'Nigger Mike's.' I was with Whitey Lewis, one of the gunman in the Rosenthal case. I heard singing coming from a transom of the Doyer Street Midnight Mission. I said to Whitey, 'I'm going into that place to see a friend of mine.' Whitey uttered a curse and said, 'I'll be waiting for your around the corner.' I wanted to see if I could do the things Madison Edwards said I could.

"A short time before, I sent my parole papers to Mr. Edwards and asked him if he would be my friend. He wrote, 'I didn't know you were running away from justice when we first met, but I was your friend then, I still am and always will be.' This did something to me, and I answered, 'I will surrender myself to God.' This was on my mind when I went into the mission.

"As I entered they were singing a hymn and I sat down to listen. In that very room a few weeks before, I had planned to lure a former pal and blow out his brains for revenge. When I heard the mission preacher say that Christ was there to receive anyone who cared to come to Him, I took a chance and went to the platform. There were only two of us who went forward. The other guy was a frowsy old fellow, full of dirt and vermin. I said, 'If you want me to pray, you had better keep that bum at the other side of the bench.' After they moved the bum over, I said, 'Lord, I don't know anything about this stuff that they hand me, but if you can do for me what you've done for Captain Edwards, prove it to me and I will serve you all the days of my life.'

George Ellis

"That night I wrote Mr. Edwards. It meant something to me to be a Christian. Every cop in town knew me and I knew what it was to be shaken down."

This was the way George Ellis described his conversion, but that came eleven years after his first contact with Madison Edwards. In those eleven years the former choir boy had become a stickup man, a burglar, a swindler, a bomb planter and a mankiller. When he left the mission that night a copy grabbed him and told him he had a nerve to go below the crook's downtown deadline. "He then hit me a smash in the jaw that shook my body more than the Spirit of Christ had already shaken it. The day before I would have killed that cop. Instead I dropped my hands, told the cop that I found Christ and that the only blow I would ever strike again would be for His cause, or in defense of a woman." The cop was unimpressed, telling him that he was the type of man who would make crooks out of angels.

If this part of the story seems rather fantastic, let George tell what happened eleven years before.

"At eighteen I came in contact with Madison Edwards. I was on a schooner called the Basantoland. It was in February, 1898, and I was a fugitive from justice. I had to get out of New York some way, and jumping aboard a bluenose schooner seemed the only way. Mr. Edwards came in his boat and took me with others ashore. When he arrived I got on the rear end, because I didn't want to see him or anyone that had religion. I had no intention of going to a religious service. I considered a religious nut the worst nut of all.

"After talking to several of the men, he came over to me. 'How are you, my brother?' he inquired. I just mumbled a few words and made an effort to leave. That didn't work.

"The next question set me off. 'Are you a Christian?' he asked. 'Do I look like a Zulu,' I shot back.

"He didn't bat an eyelash, but quietly asked, 'How are your relations with Jesus Christ?'

" 'My relations are alright,' I snapped. 'I don't want anything to do with you church people.' Then I began to rip into the churches. We were standing on the wharf at the time and I expected him to quickly drop me. Instead he asked quietly, 'Will you come up to the Bethel?' I went. That night they gave me a ditty bag full of pins, buttons and things sailors use.

"Then Mr. Edwards invited me into his office, and we talked for over an hour. I was thinking, what kind of a game is this? What is his motive? Was the ditty bag used as bait? When I left I told him I wanted nothing to do with Jesus Christ or religion. He said, 'Will you give me the privilege of writing to you?'

" 'Sure,' I answered, 'if that is going to relieve your conscience.' So I gave him a phony name. 'Just call me Bruce Wallace,' I concluded. I can't understand it, but even though I did everything but swear at him, he never lost patience. Something else I can't explain. In spite of myself, what he said went to my heart.

"I was not aware of the importance then, but on that cold February night, Madison Edwards planted the seed in my life that eventually led to my conversion. In the following years every time I thought he had forgotten, a letter arrived, addressed to Bruce Wallace. In it he would say, 'I hope and pray it will not be long before you come back. I am your friend and love you like a brother. You will always find a warm place at my home.' I cursed these letters, always afraid my companions would see them.

"The next few years I travelled all over the world, a more hardened criminal than ever. But I had promised him I would write and whatever city or country I expected to visit, I would always find a letter waiting when I arrived. They all carried the same message, 'Bruce, I am still praying for you.' When I told him I was in jail it made no difference. 'Your letter had made me sad,' he would write, 'but, oh, my boy, I still love you and will continue to pray for you wherever you wander.' "

George was arrested in Georgia for carrying explosives, had a sixteen pound ball rivetted to his legs and worked in the chain gang every day. He soon grew tired of that and escaped. Arriving back north he was arrested, but again escaped, this time going to Mexico. Here he sent a bullet through the heart of a former pal and sent another to the hospital. He was fired upon first, and carried that bullet for life. He was sentenced to death, but his plea of self defense caused the judge to reconsider and reduce his sentence to life in prison.

Still Madison's letters kept coming, even though he knew of the life sentence. "Wallace," he wrote, "I am still praying for you. I am going to see the day when you will become a Christian."

Through the help of several oil companies, he was eventually deported as an undesireable alien. He had been reduced to a skeleton. After recovering his strength he again reverted to his criminal ways, was arrested and sent to Elmira Reformatory. It was following this, his longest term in any jail, that he turned his life over to God at the Rescue Mission.

His first honest job was driving an ambulance. While serving in this capacity he was called to the Triangle Shirtwaist factory where one hundred and forty-nine girls were killed. This was followed by a nervous breakdown. He had no place to go. He was too proud to go home and his pals in crime had all left him. He wrote the Bethel Chaplain who immediately responded with the words, "Come here and I will take care of you."

"The thing that broke me up," said George, "was that Mr. Edwards and Mr. Tower brought me into their own homes and took a chance on me, when no one else would.

"He started me out by asking me to sing. That was the first time I ever sang a gospel solo. I thank God that there was such a place and such men who stuck by me in spite of rebuffs and other things I did to them. Although I drenched my hands in human blood, they never left me and finally won me to Jesus Christ.[1]

Shortly after returning to New York, George married a young widow "who believed in me no matter what anyone told her."

He worked for some years in the Doyer Street Mission and later became assistant superintendent of the Inasmuch Mission. It was at this time that Governor Glynn of new York granted him a full pardon.

George used his fine tenor voice for the glory of God. He was soon called, "The Caruso of the Bowery," a name that always remained with him. For many years he was employed by the Evangelistic Committee of New York City, particularly in the Hell's Kitchen section. From there he became a much sought after speaker, visiting almost every large city of the country.

---

[1] This writer listened to him sing at Mrs. Tower's funeral March 25, 1942. It seemed impossible that not long before he was one of America's most wanted criminals. God moves in a mysterious way, but in this case He had the help of the Bethel Chaplains.

Chapter Twenty-Four

THE STORY OF RICHARD HALSTEAD

Richard Halstead of the barge Baltic, was a sailor whose one aim in life was to have a good time. He was a likeable lad, with above average intelligence. He also had a devilish desire to shock people. Chaplain Edwards was drawn to him because of his good nature and ease of making friends. This was only the second time in his life that he had been near a religious service, but life aboard ship had become so boring that he thought maybe the Bethel would be a good place to while away some time on shore.

Chaplain Edwards drew this boy aside and an open and enlightening conversation developed. Richard apparently thought the time had arrived for him to shock his questioner, for with a good deal of embellishment he recited his moral lapses, his hard drinking, his love of gambling, and the role of women in his life. Madison heard him through, and soon Richard found he was before a man who could shock one also.

The chaplain very quietly reminded him of another young man who had the same outlook upon life, enjoying all the things he claimed to enjoy. However, after a few years his body became weak, his face bloated, his happy disposition gone, and he was left penniless and friendless. "Do you know what happened to that young men?" was the quiet question asked. "Of course you don't because it is in the Bible, the book you confess you have never read, and it was told by Jesus, the Man you do not know. But I will tell you. He ended his wild career tending hogs, the most despised and degrading job for a Jewish youth, and the only food he had was what was fed these pigs. Jesus called this a parable, and I want you to hear its teaching.

"From what you have told me, I will tell you how you will look ten years from now. Instead of being strong and vigorous you will be weak and emaciated. Instead of clear eyes and a ready wit, your eyes will be bleary and blood shot and you will have difficulty deciding where you are and how you got there. You will no longer have an attractive personality, neither will you still be able to laugh your troubles away. Instead of being well dressed you will be unkempt. Your face will no longer look fresh and clean, but scarred and wrinkled like that of an old, unclean man, unless you change your ways now before it is too late."

"Do you really believe that?"

"I not only believe it, I know it will be so. The only way you can avoid all of this is by accepting Jesus and following Him. My dear boy, I love you and God loves you and neither of us want you to become a derilect of the streets. Go back, my boy, to the Baltic, think it over, and come see me again. I am going to pray with you now, and whether you have ever done it or not, before you go to bed I want you to pray for yourself."

After leaving the Bethel, Richard said to a companion, "No one has ever talked to me like that. I can't get what he said off my mind. That isn't what I want my life to be."

That night was a sleepless one. The next day was similar to the long, weary night. He couldn't drive this future, as outlined by the chaplain, from his mind. He decided to do something about it. That evening he went to the Bethel and when the invitation was given for those who would yield their lives to Christ, his hand was raised higher than any other. Madison took those who responded into his office where he could talk and pray with them. Richard's simple prayer was, "Oh, Lord Jesus, help me to be good." He joined the Hold Fast Society, and when he left Vineyard Haven he still had that contagious smile, plus a purpose in life he had never desired before.

Three quarters of a year passed, with this youth writing to Madison as often as he could, always reminding him that he was still holding fast. He was now on the barge Stonington, and on March 16, 1911, he wrote stating that he was on his way east, and would soon be "home" at the Bethel again. "I want to leave the sea and go to Mt. Hermon school," he confided, "and prepare myself for helping others as you are."

He did come home to the Bethel, but not as was expected. The barge Stonington sprang a leak in the sound, and had to be abandoned by the crew. Richard was in the same boat with the captain, and froze to death during the ten hours before the boat drifted ashore at Nantucket.

With tears he could no longer supress, Madison wrote Boston, "This dear Hold Fast boy is lying in death here in the Bethel tonight, within a few feet of me."

The next day he clothed the boy and tenderly prepared him for burial in the Bethel cemetery lot. No father could have done more for a son. He even selected a special place for the burial—beside that of a saintly old sailor, Jimmie Williams, who had been laid there only a few months before. He felt that these two dedicated men, one old enough to be the father of the other, should be together.

A short time later, the Stonington's captains son, a chum of Richard, came to the Bethel to take his pal's place in the Hold Fast.

Chapter Twenty-Five

THE GOSPEL SKIPPERS

Some called them the "Gospel Skippers," and the Helen May the "Little Devil Chaser." These chaplains were not fair weather skippers, but fair weather or foul, were out fishing--for men. "I have learned over and over," said the chief skipper, "that if we would catch men, we must cast the line of invitation where they are. If only one man in the entire fleet would go ashore, I would go after him."

There are times when even these hardy seamen would rather be sitting before the Bethel fireplace than facing an angry sea, "But," Madison explained, "If I am to get the men I must run some risks. It is not the dangers that matter, but the one man made better."

The following experience of a stormy night was typical of many.

The storm that had begun early in the day was increasing in intensity. The strong northeast wind caused the rain to beat against the windows. The streets were quiet for most people were glad to be home on a night like this. For the two chaplains of the Bethel, however, the night was just beginning. Quietly they watched the schooners and tug boats as they scurried into the harbor. Looking at the clock on the wall, Austin saw it was time to go after the "boys." Some nights they might not have ventured forth in such rough weather, but with so many vessels at anchor, they couldn't let this opportunity go by.

Arrangements had been made for the evening, and entertainers and hostesses had already arrived. Chairs were set up and hymn books distributed. Some pages were torn and others missing from these books, for the men loved to sing and had given them hard usage. The fireplace was sending out a cheery blaze and everything was in readiness for an evening of inspiration, fellowship and refreshment.

The two missionaries began their rough trip. In spite of the weather, the men were ready and waiting to go ashore, and the Bethel boat was filled. It would take more than rough seas and rain to keep them away. Many looked forward to being "home" again, for Chaplain Edwards was the only father some of them knew; neither did they hesitate to call his devoted wife, "mother." The assistant chaplain was twenty-eight years the younger, and was looked upon by some as a "big brother."

Once ashore, the men thoroughly enjoyed their evening. Even men that had to stand watch that night were not concerned about their return trip, for as sure as the Helen May brought them in, she would get them back.

Returning to the vessels was not easy on nights like this. The larger craft were often anchored two or three miles off shore. As someone said of the engineer and pilot of the Helen May, "They plied their little craft in the dark, and densest fog, finding their way by some mysterious sense, from ship to ship, and ship to shore." As always, they returned in safety and were glad they had not allowed the weather to keep them ashore.[1]

Here is a personal account of one of these trips down harbor to return men to their vessels. "When we started back the winds were blowing a gale. Some of the vessels were two miles down harbor. Our boat plowed bravely through heavy seas that sometimes made a clean breach of water. The men were anxious to make their vessels and some were frightened. Soon all the lights went out and the steering gear became deranged and we had to rely chiefly upon the engine for steering. The men were landed with difficulty. In one instance the boat mounted upon a wave high above the deck of the vessel. The captain and his men went sprawling upon the deck. Another great wave lifted the boat and smashed it against the vessel, but without damage to the boat. All the men were finally placed aboard and the boat returned with only a few broken windows."

The Helen May in a Nor'easter

A Boston Globe article about Chaplain Tower, contained this paragraph. "So the chaplain has to be a capable boatsman and pilot of no mean ability. He must be able to lay his tossing craft alongside the towering side of a down east lumberman and put the crew aboard without damaging his boat or injuring the men. And he must locate the vessels and find his way home again."

This matter of locating vessels on the return trip was shared by the men. A recurring problem was that many of the newer men couldn't recognize their ship on a dark night. Many times a sailor would say, "I think that is my vessel," often attempting to board, only to find he was mistaken. Then came the slow circling through the fleet until the right ship was found. The Bethel boat often covered three or four miles before all men were aboard and the weary chaplains were safely tied up at their wharf.

"I am sure that if good has been done it is God's work, and

it makes me happy. I thank God that He can use me in His service, and to His name I give all the praise," said the senior Sky Pilot.

A near fatal accident occurred in 1910, again on a stormy night. While picking up men from the fleet, a large, heavy set man fell overboard. He shouted to Mr. Edwards to save him. The boat had swung off a little, and coming up, went over the man. Backing away again the unfortunate seaman came in sight and Madison got hold of him with one hand and with the other clung to the pilot house. He called for help but with the noise of the storm and the loud roar of the engine, none of the twenty men in the cabin could hear him. This was a desperate situation. The man was too heavy for him to rescue alone, and his aching arm warned him that he he could not hold on much longer, and he could get no help. Finally, by a tremendous effort he managed to reach the bell button and held it long enough to signal Austin to stop. The men on board dashed from the cabin, and it was only a matter of minutes, but it took many strong hands to pull the heavy man aboard.

With rescue accomplished, and thinking the excitement was over, all breathed a sigh of relief. The Helen May headed back to the barge, from which the man had come, in a hurry to find dry clothes and the shelter of a warm cabin. Eventually the barge was reached and the uncomfortable man put aboard--only to find it was not his! In the darkness of that stormy night, even the rescued, man couldn't distinguish his own ship. Once again he was lowered to the launch, this time with the assistance of many willing hands, and eventually landed on his own deck.

Again, Chaplain Edwards was returning from Woods Hole with his friend, Will Leach, aboard. It was night and half way across the sound a sudden, heavy fog blotted out all visibility. It was in the days when the New York steamer was still running, and they heard her fog horn every few seconds. Because of the poor visibility they were not sure of the whereabouts of the steamer, until suddenly they realized she was on top of them. To break the tension, Madison shouted, "What will we do, Willie?" By that time Will Leach was praying. He stopped long enough to shout back, "Give her full steam ahead!" Why he said that he was never sure, but they passed her bow by less than fifty feet. As the waves tossed the Helen May about, they hastily glanced up, and discovered they were so close that even the fog couldn't hide the people lining the rails.

There was one man who knew all about these chances Madison took, for he had been with him in both sunshine and storm. He was Franklin Shumway, and he wrote this tribute to the pilot's ability. "I personally have been with him when the old boat would take a wiggle and dive down apparently for the last time, and I would say to myself, 'Goodbye, Shumway, you'll never get back to town,' but somehow we always came up again."

Austin Tower was equally daring. The Rev. Haig Adadourian was with him one Christmas eve, and later wrote, "Through the darkness and deluge of rain the Helen May plowed her way down the harbor until she was outside the chops, and there with the wind breezing and the sea rising, her steering gear went out of commission. Mr. Tower found that trouble was caused by the quadrant slipping from the rudder-head and to reach the seat of the trouble he was obliged to raise a hatch on the after deck, outside of the house.

"Being unable to replace the quadrant so that it would remain in place, he stood on the open deck, holding it in place with his foot, while his son, Alden, at the wheel went through the fleet, picking up twenty-five men from the vessels. It was an hours run...with rain descending in torrents and seas breaking clear over the boat from bow to stern as she worked windward."

"I was mighty glad I went through," said Mr. Tower, "because the vessels sailed the next morning, and all the boys had received just a little Christmas cheer."

---

[1] By 1920, 25,000 men had been brought to the Bethel. Statistics are lacking on the years that followed.

Chapter Twenty-Six

A NIGHT AT THE BETHEL

The chaplain wrote of a severe gale that had lasted several nights and for once kept him ashore. The third night he decided to go to the vessels in spite of the risk involved. Almost immediately after leaving the wharf his launch was plunging wildly. To his surprise when the vessels were reached, men were lined up and waiting to board. When one captain slid down, the launch gave a quick roll and tossed him into the cabin. Another, not expecting the Helen May on such a night, came down half dressed with his shoes and coat in his hands. Madison said, "How he made it I don't know, but he got there. It was a rough time and filled everyone with excitement through the whole evening."

A critic once visited the Bethel to determine if all that he had heard was true. He was surprised when he met the chaplain for he had expected him to be dynamic and powerful, but instead found him humble and outgoing, with a smile and hearty hand shake for everyone. "At first sight," he confessed, "he hardly seemed to be the man to mingle with big, uncouth sailors. He proved, however, to be an interesting, cheerful talker, a man of superb tact and great personal influence among seamen."[1]

The evening started with the singing of gospel songs, many of the men asking for favorites, and all joining in with gusto. He listened to a simple but inspiring message given before a room full of sailors, and when an invitation was extended, at least a dozen asked for prayer and a chance to start a new life. Then at the close of the fellowship hour, the critic went away feeling the reports he had heard were definitely true.

The greatest drawing power at the mission, strange as it may seem, was the religious service. When the Helen May pulled alongside, one of the first questions was, "Will there be a meeting tonight?" Not only were these men anxious to hear a good Gospel message, but most had a problem of one sort or another and they knew the chaplains would be both understanding and sympathetic.

As soon as the boat was docked, the men made their way up the wharf to the Bethel, warm and cheerful, with the wives and daughters of the chaplains waiting to greet them. Many times there were other young ladies, a group of singers or young people who would entertain later in the evening. Now all mingled with the sailors, and voices and laughter filled the room.

Soon a voice above the din might be heard saying, "O.K., boys, pull up your chairs and we'll sing a while." Madison or Austin usually led the singing, but it could have been Captain Luce. He was present at the dedication of the building and continued to help at the Bethel as long as he was able. He also offered his services as soloist or song leader on many occasions.

In the early days a family orchestra was formed. It consisted of Helen at the organ, May keeping the rhythm with a tambourine, and Madison beating the big bass drum. The sailors loved this innovation and sang lustily on every hymn.

Among the gospel songs in the old hymnbook, were many favorites, among them, "Pull for the Shore, Sailor," "Throw out the Life Line," "Jesus, Saviour Pilot Me," and "Nearer my God to Thee." Above all, the most meaningful was "Let the Lower Lights be Burning." They could relate to that. Many were the times when on a stormy or foggy night, all eyes were strained landwards, eager to catch the glimmer of lights along the shore.

But the chaplains told of another meaning of this hymn, a meaning which came alive as they sang the verses. God our Father constantly beams His love and mercy upon us, but He

The Bethel as it appeared in 1906 showing the bass drum used by Madison

gives to us the responsibility of keeping this love-light burning in our lives for the benefit of those about us who may be tempest tossed or lost in darkness. The chaplain continued in a personal way, to tell the men that the Bethel ministry was just that--to keep the lower lights burning for them and all seamen. "Thousands have sat here as you do tonight, and are now scattered all over the world. Some are in dangerous waters. Others, whose anchor grips the solid rock that is Jesus Christ, are safe."

Following are the words of this great hymn.

> *"Brightly beams our Father's mercy*
> *From His lighthouse evermore;*
> *But to us He gives the keeping*
> *Of the lights along the shore.*
>
> *"Trim your feeble lamp my brother!*
> *Some poor seaman, tempest tossed,*
> *Trying now to make the harbor,*
> *In the darkness may be lost.*

"Let the lower lights be burning!
Send a gleam across the wave!
Some poor fainting, struggling seaman
You may rescue, you may save.

"Dark the night of sin has settled,
Loud the angry billows roar.
Eager eyes are watching, longing,
For the lights along the shore."

    Chaplain Tower had a reason to be concerned about keeping the lower lights burning. The Bethel lights were kept burning every night of the week, but also as he spoke there was a light blinking on the breakwater in the harbor. The breakwater was built by the state in 1910. It was an oil light, and there must have been some difficulty in keeping it going for in 1911 Captain Edwards was appointed light-keeper. This job fell upon his assistant who was to keep the oil tanks replenished, as well as to keep it burning at all costs during windy and stormy weather. This was often a difficult task, as the tanks had to be filled from a small skiff, and rough water and the rocks of the jetties were dangerous obstacles.[2]

    After the song service ended, there followed prayer and lessons from the scriptures. The format of the service varied from night to night, but always produced the same results--changed lives. It did not contain the beauty found in formal worship, but it did possess a strength not felt in most churches.

    A time for personal testimonies was always included. Some were anxious to tell what God had done for them, while others were ill at ease, and it probably took more courage on their part to speak than it did to stand watch in a raging sea. One young man said timidly, "I never got up and confessed before, but I do tonight. Pray for me that I, too, may be a true man." Others took courage from what he had said. "I'm glad I'm on the Lord's side," said a second man, "pray for me." One could see that it was difficult for him, too, for drops of perspiration stood on his brow. Another with more poise, followed. "Since I was last here I have had a severe trial, but when I saw my badge I knew the "Hold Fast" boys were praying for me and it helped me to overcome."

Occasionally Madison would read a written testimony which came to him in a letter. Two of these follow. "When I felt lonely on the sea I took to reading the Testament you gave me, and the purity and sublime beauty of that book gave me pleasure hitherto unknown and filled me with a happiness and contentment never dreamed of before." This man could have been an officer.

Another found great satisfaction also. "When I went on board the vessel the other night I read my Bible and knelt and asked God to take away my sins. I know my prayer was heard for I have been so happy ever since."

Next came the question, "Are there any who would like to take Christ as their Pilot?" Without any urging many hands were lifted. "It was a sight to make a Christian heart rejoice to see the uplifted hands," wrote a Vineyard Gazette reporter. Meeting with the chaplain in his office followed for those who had decided for Christ or who wanted counsel with him.

The little office would often be crowded with young men who wanted to begin again. This was not the only place, however, where confessions were made. It was a common sight to see one or the other chaplain sitting before the Bethel fireplace, listening to a young man as he confessed his mistakes and expressed his desire to live better. A loving arm would be placed about him as they prayed together.

Franklin P. Shumway told of hearing Madison praying; "Oh God, You have heard John and what he says about himself. Can you do anything for a fellow like him? Then John and he and God get together, and I tell you, brethren, John is a different man when he leaves that room—"

Parents all over the world were praying for the Bethel and its chaplains, happy in the thought that eventually their sons, and other boys like them, would come under the influence of these good men. Sometimes that contact came late. An example of that occurred when an eighteen year old Norwegian boy was killed in a fall into the hole of his barge while anchored in Vineyard Haven harbor. Madison buried him in the Bethel lot, gathered his few belongings and sent them to his parents in Norway. Back came a letter from the mother saying that he had run away from home, "But," she added, "I thought that somewhere he would come in contact with God's people." He had.

The fellowship hour at the Bethel varied from night to night. Many local people as well as church groups, youth organizations, and even children were eager to help in entertaining and the serving of refreshments. A period of recreation was often included with many games available. Many enjoyed the fireplace where they toasted marshmallows, popped corn, or just chatted and exchanged sea stories. But when Madison announced an evangelistic candy pull, all knew there was fun ahead.

For this candy pull, the ladies cooked the ingredients together to just the right consistency, then the men buttered their hands and taking a portion, began to pull the candy. Hilarious excitement often followed, as the men tried to quickly handle the hot mass, and then keep working it until it had cooled and hardened enough to be snipped into small pieces. How stuck up some would get! All were left in a jovial mood.

When refreshments were served they usually consisted of ice cream and homemade cakes. On one occasion when a fleet had been held in the harbor for some time, it was decided for a change of pace to serve clam chowder. Preparations went on all day--shucking clams, peeling potatoes, etc. until several gallons of steaming hot chowder were in readiness. Late that afternoon the wind changed, up went the sails, and every ship left the harbor. It was rumored that many Vineyard Haven families enjoyed clam chowder for supper that night.

On a cold December night, Madison produced a large plum

pudding which caused the sailors to break forth with cheers.

Mrs. Ruth Eldridge White, with a group of other young women of the town, were always interested in the Bethel work, and often offered their talents in the entertainment field. She wrote, "I remember how exciting it was to help. First there was a religious service, led by Mr. Edwards, with daughter Helen at the organ...we joined with them in "Pull for the Shore, Sailor," and "Let the Lower Lights Be Burning." After the service we young ladies would 'elocute' a few selections, sing duets or play a violin solo. After that I recall passing coffee, home made cake, and presenting the comfort bag to each sailor present.

"Those of us who know the remarkable work of the Seaman's Bethel have a feeling of lofty pride in the achievement of the service. It is a pride that soars, for there is no measure to the power and influence emanating from that lovely mission."

Among those who through the years entertained the seamen were Lucy and Sarah Adams. They were "little people," and in their youth worked for P. T. Barnham. They were bridesmaids at Tom Thumb's wedding. In later years they appeared in various parts of the country in their own show, which consisted of pantomines and tableaux illustrating hymns and Bible stories. They were an added attraction for the sailors, both at the Bethel and the Marine Hospital.[3]

---

[1] Readers of this book may picture the men of whom we write as those in sailor's uniforms, or maybe the big, burly and uncouth men whom the critic had in mind. They were neither. They were young men, often still in their teens, and came from the coastal towns and villages scattered along the coast of Maine, New Brunswick and Nova Scotia. They were clean cut, friendly and with a youthful outlook on life.

[2] Austin continued with this responsibility until an electric blinker was installed in 1922.

[3] Sarah was dead when this writer became pastor of their church, but Lucy was still living. She was a beautiful soul, but a firey little person. Many times her pastors received a tongue lashing when she thought they were no longer orthodox in their theology.

Chapter Twenty-Seven

SHIPMATES AT REST

A separate book could be written on the touching stories in connection with many of those now resting in God's Acre. Young and old, known and unknown and from far and near, all lie together in the shadow of the lighthouse.

Madison received a letter from Albo, Finland. It was written by a retired seaman, who on many earlier occasions had visited the Bethel. His son, Gustave Gunner Mannerstrom, who had followed his father's footsteps, had been badly injured in the destruction of his ship while in the vicinity of the Vineyard, and was brought to the Marine Hospital. In spite of his painful condition, he had refused to enter the life boat until all others were safely aboard. As a result pneumonia developed and he died a hero, who gave his life for others. He was twenty-nine years old. With loving care he was tenderly laid to rest in God's Acre. The father concluded his letter with these words. "I know that my dear son is alright, especially when he died in your care. God bless you and the Bethel. You have my thanks forever."

On the whole, most seamen were not known for their saintliness, although many were devout men. Eighty year old Jimmie Williams was one of the latter. He was confined to the Marine Hospital for a long period of time, but never missed an opportunity to attend the religious services held there by the chaplains. Both Madison and Austin spent much time with him, and the affection they had for each other was well known. When Jimmie passed away in 1910 the missionaries felt they had lost a father. Jimmie made it clear long before, that he did not want his body shipped back to England. He added, "please bury me in God's Acre. I want to be beside my mates, and whatever money I have left I want you to use it for the Bethel work." He left $460.00, not much to be sure, but for this man it meant a life of sweat and toil. Madison used some of that money for an engraved headstone--one of the few in the Bethel lot.

Not long after Jimmie's passing, Richard Halstead, whose story is already recorded in this volume, rested in the undertaking parlor, with a broken hearted chaplain making arrangements for his burial. He had given Richard so much fatherly care and counsel, that now in death he still felt that close relationship. He thought again of Jimmie Williams, and again of Richard who wanted to prepare himself for Christian work, and felt they should be together, so they were placed side by side.

In 1915 another sad assignment came to Madison. Among his Hold Fast members were two young brothers from Nova Scotia, Earl and Fred McLaughlin. They died at sea only a month apart. Fred was twenty-two, and the vessel on which he was a crew member arrived in Vineyard Haven harbor in the middle of June. Madison tells the story of his death in his own informal way.

"He was leaning over the side of a boat attempting to secure something, lost his balance and was drowned. I said to the captain, 'I must drag for the body,' but he wouldn't let me, saying he would drag the next day. I knew that would be too late as the tide would turn and wash the body away. I wrote his mother asking what I should do when the body was recovered. She answered, 'Send it home by all means.' It was ten days before the body was found, and by that time his mother had written saying, 'Let him rest in Vineyard Haven, the place he loved so much. I feel there is no better place in the world than there.'

"A month later his brother, Earl, left home. He too, was drowned, and lost at sea. I had a letter from the mother and she said, 'All the boys are going to war but my two boys will never come back.' But the thought that we had a beautiful

Fred McLaughlin at left with other crewmen

place to bury Fred gave her comfort. 'Can't you put a beautiful rose on his grave?' I told her he would also have a little stone, such as all sailors had. After hunting awhile I found a white stone and I have been bleaching it a little whiter."[1]

---

[1] Until the death of Chaplain Tower in 1961, God's Acre was carefully tended. Never a week passed but what he went there to mow the grass, trim the shrubs or place memorial flowers. After Mr. Tower's death the Boston Seaman's Friend Society paid for perpetual care, and the grounds continue well-kept. Ocassionally some friend of seamen remembers those buried there with plants or flowers.

It is interesting to note that a cross was carved in the stone at the grave of each sailor whose name was unknown. There is a cross on the first two stones marking the graves of those who perished in the Portland Storm. They were the two unidentified bodies from the Island City wrecked at Oak Bluffs. The third from that storm is that of William McElweis of St. Andrews, New Brunswick.

The complete list of sailors buried in both the Bethel lot and Marine Hospital Cemetery, in so far as they can be obtained, will be found at the end of this volume.

Chapter Twenty-Eight

DRAMA OF PEACE AND WAR

December 17, 1912, marked Madison's twentieth year at Vineyard Haven, and he had promised the seamen he would have something special for them. Others had plans also, of which he was unaware. Local friends of the Bethel planned to invade his meeting that very night with gifts, and refreshments sufficient for all. For several days Mrs. Sydna Eldridge and Mrs. Willis Hancock had quietly rounded up neighbors and friends and at the appointed time seventy-five were in attendance. Were it not for a boisterous storm which kept the number of both seamen and citizens down, the Bethel would not have been able to hold them all.

When Mr. Edwards returned from gathering sailors from the harbor and saw the assembled crowd, he was genuinely surprised and said, "Why, I don't understand this. I don't know what to do." "Don't worry," was the response, "We'll tell you."

Helen Tower read the 91st Psalm, and Mrs. Gifford offered one of her fervent prayers. The designated speakers then extended their heartiest congratulations and appreciation for the splendid service he had given in turning hundreds of sailors into the straight and narrow path. Mrs. Eldridge said her first real impression of Mr. Edwards came when she realized that he was a man doing good because he loved to do good, and served his fellowmen with no thought of remuneration.

In 1916 there circulated a false rumor that the Boston Seaman's Friend Society was moving the Bethel to Monument Beach at the west end of the Cape Cod Canal.

This arose because Madison was to be temporarily assigned there, to determine if there was need of establishing a work in that area.

On the eve of their departure, October 31, 1916, a surprise party was held for them. About fifty friends walked in on him once again while he was conducting a service. Mrs. Eldridge had again interested friends and had refreshments prepared. Miss Annie Gonyon sang, the Misses Renear rendered vocal and violin solos and Miss Fairbrother gave a reading. Nelson Luce, John Crowell and Mrs. Eldridge each expressed their appreciation of the work, and extended their best wishes for the new venture. The Bethel was filled and the words spoken were, "Mr. and Mrs. Edwards, we love you and want to tell you so."

The next day the Edwards family left, taking with them the Helen May and their son, Howard and his family. He was to be the engineer of the launch, thus leaving Austin with the little Aransas.

The canal reading room was small and rather poorly equipped. It also turned out to be a miserable and unproductive winter. From early January to March 20 the Helen May was frozen solid so that very little could be accomplished. Also two large steamers had sunk across the channel so ships could not get through. Between the ice and the submerged steamers, the work he wanted to do was impossible. It was mostly the few who could walk over the ice to his home that made up his congregation. As though this was not enough, Austin, on one of his visits to his father-in-law, broke his wrist trying to crank his car. This slowed the already limited work in Vineyard Haven.

The merchant sailors were among the first to enlist in World War I in 1917. Many chose the navy, but some enlisted in the army. Among the latter were two brothers, Arlington and Parlee Ward, of Rockport, New Brunswick. They were both members of the Hold Fast Brotherhood and were friends of the Tower family. It was a homecoming every time their vessel anchored in Vineyard Haven harbor, and they had

Helen May frozen in at canal

a chance to visit with Austin. After their enlistment they went to the front with the Canadian troops. At the battle of the Somme, Arlington, the older of the two boys was instantly killed. Before the battle ended, Parlee was struck in the leg by a piece of flying shrapnel, which later necessitated amputation. Parlee had married only a short time before leaving Canada, and most of the information we have of the tragic weeks that followed his injury, were letters sent to his young bride. They appeared in the Sackville, New Brunswick, newspaper, from which are taken the following excerpts.

"Dear Wife, ... I suppose you saw where the Canadians figured largely in our recent victories. Well, I happened to be one of the boys that day. I didn't stand it long, for a shrapnel shell burst at my feet and broke my right leg...but the worst of it was that I couldn't get carried out, so had to stay in a shell hole all day. The explosive made my leg so bad that I have had to have it taken off above the knee. But don't worry...I am a lot better off than a lot of poor chaps I see.

"I have suffered. I hardly believed a person could feel so much pain, but I have not failed...I wish I knew where Arlie was...don't know if he would be in the drive or not. Hope he wasn't."[2]

After returning to Canada he wrote Austin: "I have been

Parlee and Arlington Ward

fitted with an artificial leg...Guess I will be able to get along with it after a time, but it's hard work, though. You see, the thing doesn't understand starboard and port so I have a hard time to navigate it.

"You know, Austin, The Bethel did me a lot of good. I know I haven't lived up to my obligations as I should have done, and then I would think of you people and be heartily ashamed of myself. I only wish I had more of its influence."

Along with the war came the influenza epidemic of 1918 which resulted in the closing of all public places, including the Bethel. This lasted for eight weeks, during which time the Helen May was kept busy taking the medical examiner and quarantine doctors to the many vessels, bringing officers ashore for provisions and returning them again, and carrying mail, messages and telegrams back and forth to the vessels.

The following year while Austin was vacationing in Canada, he received a letter from Madison with the following information. "On Sept. 9th I had one of my spells with my heart while pumping out the Helen May. I called Dr. Mayhew and after two hours I felt better." This was one of the numerous light heart attacks he had had, and would continue to have.

This year marked his thirtieth year as chaplain of the Bethel and in honor of this event, the Boston Seaman's Friend Society presented him with a gold watch.

The winter of 1920-21 brought another season of severe storms and many ship wrecks.

The schooner, W.W.H. White, left Vineyard Haven harbor and sailed into oblivion. Two of her crew had joined the Hold Fast the previous night.

In the middle of March the schooner, Isaiah B. Stetson, Captain William Reicker, was shipwrecked on Handkerchief Shoals in a southwest gale. He told how four of his men lost their lives.

"I ordered the men to take to the masts. Mate Nelson McKay and seaman Manford Nickerson reached the top of the forward deck house when they were washed overboard. Seaman Emden Ellis climbed aloft and I thought he was safe, but he tried to cross on a spring stay from one mast to another and he went over when the water caught him. I had cook Robert Hodgson with me in the fore rigging, but he tried to climb a bit higher when the schooner sank and I lost him."

For fourteen hours the two remaining men clung wildly to the pitching mast until they were frozen into security. There they remained until rescued by the Coast Guard Cutter Acushnet. This crew was at the Bethel the night before, and several of those now gone, and the captain had taken part in the service.

In October of 1924, the ill-fated schooner, Susan B., anchored in the harbor and as always Captain Bishop and as many of the crew as had shore leave, spent their evenings at the Bethel. With the captain was Mrs. Bishop, who had sailed with him for twenty-seven years, and an eighteen year old neice. After leaving Vineyard Haven they ran into a heavy westerly gale and snowstorm. The ship sprang a leak and all were forced to take to the small yawl. For fifty-two hours they were afloat in this small boat, the captain wet from a mishap in jumping from the schooner. At one point they spotted a steamer, but were not seen by them. When another ship was seen, many hours later, they fastened a blanket to an oar which attracted the attention of the lookout, and their long, agonizing ordeal was over.

---

[1] He was not only unaware that his brother was in the same battle, but he had not received the news of his death.

Chapter Twenty-Nine

"CAPTAIN EDWARDS HAS GONE ALOFT"

Saturday night, August 14, 1926 was very windy. Madison hadn't been well for some years, and this night he was restless. Suddenly he and Ella heard strange noises outside. Was someone trying to gain access to the second floor porch, outside their bedroom window? Madison sat up and Ella hurried to the window. Nothing unusual was apparent and she went back to bed. The excitement was of short duration, but it had been enough to trigger another of Madison's heart spells. He alerted Ella, and taking note of his breathing and color, immediately summoned the doctor and her daughter, Helen. These sudden night time calls had come with increasing frequency of late. This would be the last.

Early that summer Alfred Shelley of the Boston society visited Vineyard Haven. He was astounded at what he saw. "He retains his old sweet and loving spirit," he wrote, "but he has changed considerably." Yet he found Madison still dreaming of improvements to his beloved Bethel. Actually he wanted a new building, a modern structure that would be adequate for every need. "I hope I shall live to see it," he said.

Friday, August 13, was his birthday. He was seventy-four years old. The day was a quiet one with a number of sailors and other well wishers dropping by to offer their congratulations, and refreshments were served. He enjoyed every moment, but grew tired before the day ended. The next day, feeling quite well, he made known a desire to see a part of the island he had not visited for some time. He returned from the trip bright and happy. Before going to bed he remarked, "I may go to the tabernacle service in the morning." Instead, on that Sunday morning he slipped quietly into the Tabernacle Eternal.[1]

For some reason Austin Tower's diary was blank during the period that followed, and Chaplain Shelley leaves the only account we have. "Sunday morning, just before dawn," he said, "seemed to be the center of the great drama of life and love...Around him were gathered his wife and family. He was unconscious. Held up in the strong arms of his son-in-law, the friend I admired and loved, who had himself been touched with the fire of love from the altar of faith, had entered into the haven of eternal rest, leaving behind a beautiful past."

An awesome responsibility now rested upon the new chaplain. He prepared the following message to convey to seamen and friends the sad news. "It is with great sorrow because of the loss of our beloved father and Chaplain, that we are striving to carry on the work which he, because of his call to his home above, has left behind. We are praying that God's blessing will continue to rest upon the little Bethel at Vineyard Haven and that many a soul shall yet be led to the Lord Jesus Christ." No one could more effectively fulfill that mission than this devoted Christian, so recently made Superintendent, and his wife, Helen, who became a most faithful assistant.

Messages of condolence continued to pour in for weeks for news of his death was slow in reaching many scattered throughout the world. Harold B. Hunting, who was aware of this tremendous response, made the statement, "From Maine to Florida, from Boston to Yokohama, sailor lads told of Captain Edwards, and from all over the world the prayer rose to our Father in Heaven, 'God bless Captain Edwards. Grant him safe harbor at last.' " Professor Charles A. S. Dwight knew that he had reached that safe harbor, but said it differently and in a language all sailors understood, "Captain Edwards has now gone aloft."

Madison lived what he preached. He was as honest in his

religious pronouncements as he was in his dealings with men. His type of persuasiveness always convinced sincere seekers. He had one message and one only, and he lived by it and the men knew it and responded. As one sailor said, "He was the most genuine kind of a Christian I have ever met."

In 1892 Madison wrote in his diary, "I want a firmer trust in God, that when death shall come I will be ready to face Him." The time had come and he was ready.

---

[1] The tabernacle spoken of by Madison was the Martha's Vineyard Campmeeting Tabernacle at Oak Bluffs.

Chapter Thirty

A WANDERER

Uno Iverson was born in Greenland, but spent most of his early life in Denmark. He had the fair hair and ruddy complexion of the Scandinavian. When quite young he began his seafaring life, and his adventurous spirit drew him to the United States. For many years he was in the coastal trade, often stopping at the Bethel. In 1924 he made a decision to live more fully for Christ, and joined the Hold Fast Brotherhood. He soon sailed away, and for more than a year a letter or card would come to the Bethel signed only Uno. Apparently he had not given this name as the chaplain began to think someone was playing a game of guess who, for there was never a last name or address given. Uno eventually returned to the Bethel and the mystery was cleared up. Uno got as big a laugh out of this story as Austin did.

He was a rugged, outdoor individual common among the people of the North Sea. He was active in scouting, and that interest always remained with him. At one time he sailed to Cuba and the San Blas Islands off Panama. He became very friendly with the Indians there, teaching the young boys scout lore, and helping the tribe in many ways.

In 1929, Uno arrived at Vineyard Haven wishing to stay for a while. Austin offered him a room at the Bethel, and he did part time work there, and other odd jobs when available.

His roaming spirit got the best of him, and the lure of the San Blas Island became so strong that he decided to visit his old Indian friends.

Uno had no fear of the sea. In the winter of 1930, he embarked alone in a rowboat for Nantucket Island, about thirty miles from the Vineyard. He made it, and returning wearing a smile of satisfaction.

In the summer of 1931, he was making preparations to leave for the south. He bought a small sailboat which he named Tisbury. On one side of the sail he painted a map of Martha's Vineyard, and on the other drew a picture of the sun, with the words, "Sunny South" around it. It was to be a leisurely journey. To supplement the canned goods he would carry, he planned to catch fish, and gather nuts, berries and mushrooms. Austin helped with the final touches to the boat, loading supplies, and even slipping in stamped envelopes and cards, that he might keep him informed of his progress.

Uno Iverson just before leaving Vineyard Haven for the San Blas Islands—1932

He set sail on October 14, but the next day he returned with a broken mast. Undaunted by this mishap, he secured another mast, and set sail again the same day in his fifteen foot sailboat. His going was smooth enough until he went ashore in New Jersey, where he was taken to jail while his boat was searched for liquor. Because of his very broken English, his independence, and unique way of living he was often misunderstood.

The first rough weather he encountered was off the coast of Delaware, where he was forced to beach his boat and watch helplessly while the waves beat over her and gradually filled her with sand. On Christmas eve he was driven ashore again in a northwest gale and had to abandon his boat for forty-eight hours. Eventually he received assistance from the Coast Guard and was on his way once more.

"Perhaps you would like to know how I spent Christmas Eve," he wrote. "I waded ashore from my boat and struck out for some pines. First I made a fire and then built a lean-to and prepared something to eat. I hardly know what to name it, but it consisted mostly of mushrooms and berries that I roasted over the fire. Black walnuts were my desert, and I made sassafras tea to warm me, then to bed. The moon was full and the stars were bright, and the woods did look pretty to me."

Then came the shocking news from Broadwater, Virginia, by way of a letter written by Mrs. Richard Carpenter whose son had spent some time on the Vineyard. She wrote:

"A man arrived here about two weeks ago stating that he was from Vineyard Haven, Massachusetts, but refused to give his name. He said he lived here in a cabin, but was in a small skiff about fifteen feet long, equipped with a sail. He was thirty-nine years old, he said, was of medium height, light sandy hair, and was bound for Florida.

"On January 19 he bought a few eatables from a local store and left in his boat. About one mile away, out in the inlet which puts in from the ocean the boat capsized and as there was no one nearby he apparently drowned. Four days later two fishermen, returning from a clamming trip found the boat and raised it far enough to note no one was in it. Most of his belongings were lashed fast with rope, but some came ashore. It was reported that a letter was found adrift with the name Iverson on it. His body has not been found to date."

The question arises, why was this physically strong man, so accustomed to the sea, unable to save himself? Was he badly injured? Was he continuing his journey, or perhaps going fishing? He had left a bag, containing letters mostly from Denmark, on shore. It hardly seemed possible that he would have left these letters, had he not intended to return. They did, however, leave no doubt about his identity.

This was a man who liked to be alone. He died alone. Maybe this is as he would have had it.

Chapter Thirty-One

A NEW LAUNCH AND ANOTHER EXPLOSION

In January 1930, after thirty-eight years of valiant service the Helen May was retired. In March of the same year the new launch, to be named after the Bethel's first chaplain, arrived at her berth. She was a strongly built craft and her spacious cabin could accommodate fifty men. Austin Tower went to Jonesport, Maine, to the boat yard of William Frost to bring her down the coast. An old friend of the Bethel, Captain Warren White of Harrington, Maine, accompanied him. Because of his fifty-one years as a coasting skipper he was well acquainted with the inshore passages.

The dedication took place on June 3, 1930. The presentation of the launch was made by Rev. Francis A. Poole, and Mr. Gardiner E. Thorpe, Chaplain of the Boston Bethel, led the service of dedication. The final words of this beautiful service were, "To the memory of Madison Edwards, revered and loved by seamen the world around and honored by all who knew him, we dedicate this boat, in the name of the Father and of the Son and of the Holy Spirit. Amen."

The U.S. Coast Guard was represented by Chief Boatswain's Mate, John H. Kitilla, who was in charge of a detail of seamen. The sailors were also represented by Captain Nelson Luce.

"On January 9, 1934, an explosion and fire occurred on the Madison Edwards. It was a sad disaster, but how fortunate that there were no passengers on board and no lives lost." This was Austin Tower's modest account of a disaster that shook the Vineyard Haven waterfront.

The explosion took place about 4:30 p.m. A half hour

New Madison Edwards – Capt. Warren White, left and Austin Tower as they arrived at Vineyard Haven

earlier, the chaplain had left the Bethel to take on fuel for a later trip, after having a busy day in the harbor. Captain J. L. Publicover of the Laura Annie Barnes, explained the activity of the day.

"While at Vineyard Haven I had the misfortune of breaking our windlass and had to get a machinist to come aboard to work on it. My motor boat was broken down, so Mr. Tower offered to bring the workman to and from the vessel. It was during these trips that an explosion occurred that caused the destruction of the Madison Edwards. Mr. Tower had a very narrow escape--in fact, I don't see how he got out of that cabin alive."

The chaplain had just finished filling the boat's gasoline tank. Realizing the danger of fumes, he went to the engine room and cranked the motor by hand, thinking this would prevent sparks often caused by the electric self-starter. During this time Captain Ralph Packer, manager of the Texas Company, held the boat near the dock by a painter. The motor started without incident, and the chaplain signalled to cast off. After freeing the boat, Capt. Packer turned to replace the gasoline hose, when a terrific explosion occurred aboard the launch. The skiff, carried on top of the boat was blown onto the wharf, striking him in the back and knocking him down, but without injury.

By this time the Madison Edwards was ablaze, the flames shooting high above the cabin that had been blown open. Austin, who had been in the pilot house, emerged amidst the flames, and though badly shaken, managed to throw a line to the pier, drawing the boat near enough for him to leap to safety. The boat them drifted to the corner of the dock setting a section afire. This was extinguished by Capt. Packer, and he closed the valve on the pipe leading from the tanks to the dock. With a boat hook he pushed the boat clear, and she drifted off.

It was then they discovered that Prince, the Newfoundland dog that was a constant companion of the chaplain, was still on board, apparently too frightened to leap overboard. Those on shore pleaded with him to jump, but he remained there until Osborne Tower arrived, and upon hearing his familiar voice, jumped and swam ashore.

All this happened in a short space of time, and at this point the fire department had arrived. They found it impossible to put water on the boat as this forced her further away. Erford Burt rowed to the launch and pushed her to the electric company wharf, where willing hands made her fast. Before the blaze could be controlled the wraps burned off and she was set adrift again. Once more a rowboat was put out, this time with Erford Burt and Chaplain Tower aboard, who made a line fast to the stern bitt and again hauled her to the wharf. Both of these trips were hazardous, as there was a full tank of gas, as well as several five gallon cans stored below. Again secured, the flames were finally extinguished.

Following is an excerpt from a letter written by Mrs. Tower to her daughter, Miriam, in training at the Children's Hospital at the time, regarding the tragedy.

"I don't know whether you read an account today of dad's awful accident. Oh, I am so thankful he didn't get hurt. It is just a miracle for which we must thank the dear Lord. He went over to Captain Packer's wharf to get gasoline last night. After he had filled his tanks he cast off and started his motor when he heard a strange noise and turned around to see the boat all in flames. The explosion took off the roof and the skiff, lashed on top, landed right side upon the wharf. When dad came to his senses he got out...She is very badly burned, but we know nothing yet. They will wait for the insurance agent. We are all about sick. Poor Prince was aboard and had his hair badly scorched before Obie could get him to jump over. As it happened, Obie was home at the time, and when the fire whistle blew went down at once."

One side of the Madison Edwards had to be completely rebuilt, and other repairs made. After the completion of this work, the Madison Edwards and the chaplain, were again busy in their service to seamen.[1]

---

[1] As with the Helen May, the end also had to come to the Madison Edwards--at least as far as her work for the Seaman's Bethel was concerned. In 1952 she was sold to the Hagen Construction Co. of New York which was operating in South America. She was freighted to the Amazon River where she was to be used to transport workmen to various bases on the river.

Chapter Thirty-Two

A NOBLE DAUGHTER OF THE VINEYARD

"Austin," Helen called one morning, "I've had a vision! It wasn't a dream! It was real, oh, so real! It was a vision --- God's answer to my prayer!"

Helen Tower had been in poor health for the last few years. As she became more confined to her home, and often to her bed, she spent much time reading her Bible and reliving the past. She knew she would never again be active in the Bethel work that had been so much a part of her life, and in her humble way, began to wonder if she had fulfilled the task the Lord had given her to do. This weighed upon her mind, until in a most sincere and fervent prayer, she asked God to give her some assurance. The answer came in this unusual vision.

In this vision she paused at a window of her home, high on Mt. Aldworth, from which one could get a full view of the harbor. She did this often for the harbor with its ships and sailors was always upon her mind. But this was more than a pause, for there in the harbor was the most beautiful ship she had ever seen. It was a gleaming white ship; her sails were full and the sun shining upon them made them fairly glisten. The clear blue sky and shining water added to the brilliance of the scene. She was about to go to the phone in her excitement, to tell a friend not to miss this unusual sight, when the ship began to fade. She watched, spellbound until it was gone and in its place appeared an equally beautiful black craft. Still she watched, while a third ship appeared, this one of gold. As the third ship faded, a huge golden cross appeared over the harbor, as if suspended from Heaven, shedding a soft glow all about it. From just behind the cross emerged a few men, then more and more, until they formed a long line, streaming from the cross, and they kept coming in ever increasing numbers. Helen watched excitedly until this, too, faded.

It was later, with face aglow, that she told others of her experience, and what it meant to her. The three ships represented the many vessels which had come into the harbor through the years, carrying sailors of various races, creeds and colors. The gold ship could only represent the Christian sailors who had felt the influence of the Bethel, before losing their lives. The men streaming from the cross were the much loved sailor boys, who had been led to Christ through the Bethel work, of which she had been a significant part. She now had the assurance that hers had indeed been a fruitful life.

Helen as the daughter of Madison Edwards, helped entertain sailors from childhood, and as soon as she was able, played the piano at the meetings. In her early teens she knew how to deal with these men of the sea, and in 1901 she entered Northfield Seminary, Northfield, Massachusetts, to study how to become more effective in Christian work. Madison always called her his assistant.

In answering a discouraging letter from Austin, who was studying at Mt. Hermon, we discover she was very much like her mother spiritually. She wrote, "I did worry most terribly at first, but I prayed the best I knew how and each time I rose from my knees there seemed to rest upon me a most wonderful peace. I knew that God had begun to answer me. If He does not keep His precious promises to us it will be the first time in all these thousands of years that He has failed. For some reason he has seen fit to try you, but don't get discouraged...I still trust His promises. God is awfully good to me, and if He had never given me anything else but your love for me, a whole life-time of praise would not be sufficient."

She was a capable and fun loving person. After receiving a message that his mother was dying, a local telegraph operator came to the Bethel seeking transportation to the mainland.

Austin and Helen Tower before the fireplace of their home

Madison was off Island, and the weather looked bad, but Helen offered to take him. So with Helen as pilot and Austin, now home from Mt. Hermon, as engineer, and in spite of heavy ice off Nobska, they arrived in time for the train. Half way home they were caught in a snow storm, but Helen, steering by compass, brought the boat safely to the Bethel wharf.

Although most of their evenings were spent at the Bethel, Austin and Helen were devoted parents to their four children, and found time for family activities. The whole family entered into the Bethel work. The two boys were much help to their father, and in later years the youngest daughter took over as pianist.

Helen took over much of the writing, including the quarterly reports to the Society, and many personal letters. There was a great deal of correspondence with the many sailors who visited the Bethel, especially among the Hold Fast members. Each year there were printed cards, carrying the chaplain's special New Year's greeting. Hundreds of these were sent out, all addressed and stamped by hand. The children often shared in this task.

On Sunday, March 22, 1942, this truly humble but great missionary, passed away at her home. She was only fifty-eight, but she did more good in her short life than many who lived to be a hundred. Her funeral was held at the Bethel with Rev. John C. Vernon of Christ Methodist Church officiating, and was buried in Oak Grove cemetery. George Bradley Ellis sang at the funeral, and followed with this touching tribute.

"Looking back through the years I can still picture Mrs. Tower the first time we met at the Bethel, back in 1901. I was a young man from a dead-end street of New York City, bitter against the Church, schooled in the ways of the wolf-pack. And there in the Bethel she sat at the piano and played the hymns of the Church that I hated. But cynical as I was, I was compelled to realize that there was a sincerity personified and that it had attracting force...She learned the art of prayer early in life and she had a unique gift of holding on to God and pleading the cause of some wayward boy or man that she was interested in.

"When I finally made the start for God...she prayed the Heavenly Father that He might use me in His service...She encouraged me with her playing and her prayers, and that little helping hand of Helen Tower sent me out to sing the Gospel all over the country of ours. Into prisons, jails, penitentiaries, and hospitals I have carried the message of Him who died for the sinner, knowing all the time Mrs. Tower was behind me with her prayers.

"I shall miss her as a great strong heart who loved the erring with a passionate love, yearning for them as the good mother that she was, trusting that they might find Him who died for them.

"I am today a richer and better Christian for having known Mrs. Tower, and the things that I have done in the musical way have been possible because she saw beneath the rough exterior of my makeup a spark divine that needed to be fanned into a flame for Him, and she just went and did that thing."

And these words from a tribute of Mrs. Ruth Eldridge White: "The name of Helen Edwards Tower reaches to the far corners of the earth for she touched with her kindly hand the hearts of the needy men of the sea.

"We, her contemporaries, who knew her so well, share and honor her memory as one of the noblest of Vineyard daughters."

Chapter Thirty-Three

A LIFE OF COMPASSION AND LOVE

Austin Tower wrote much of what he called, "The round of little things." Actually, all were not little, but included the activities that came within his field of service, and often beyond. Space will not permit but a few of these activities, taken primarily from his diary. "Went to Handkerchief lightship, and took from the six masted schooner, the W. L. Douglas, the mate who was badly hurt. One leg was severed from his body, and the other badly broken. Conveyed him to the hospital."

A schooner bound for Grenfell's Mission on the Labrador with supplies and livestock came into the harbor with broken machinery. Every day counted in order to reach Labrador, unload the cargo and return before the weather would make the return trip impossible. Austin secured the necessary parts and a blacksmith, and both worked until the job was finished. It was 4 a.m. before the chaplain reached home.

While bound down harbor the chaplain noticed the schooner, Lillian Kerr's boat in trouble. He immediately went to their assistance, and found the boat had sprung a leak and the men had nothing with which to bail. The provisions, just purchased, were hurriedly removed, and taking on the two men, towed the boat to shore. Night was approaching, the sea rough, and if the men had not been rescued, a tragedy may have resulted.[1]

The cabin boat in which crippled Charles Hamilton, a former Marine Hospital patient, lived, capsized while being launched after repairs. It was moved to the Bethel beach, and he was taken care of at the Bethel for several weeks. In the meantime the chaplain, with the help of others, put the boat in shape again. When Captain Hamilton died a few years later, he was buried in the Bethel lot.

The "round of little things" continued day after day. Helping men and ships in danger was only a part of his work. Much time was devoted to those in spiritual danger, and he never missed an opportunity that would result in changing men's lives.

Joe Allen of the Vineyard Gazette wrote, "Religious services are held regularly by the chaplain, who preaches and prays with the simple fervor of a man who finds God in the common things of life and who drives home his spiritual lessons with the salty language that his listeners can understand and appreciate."

Marine Hospital, Vineyard Haven

Services were held at the Marine Hospital, on board ship and on shore, and he conducted the funeral services of many of the sailors who were buried in the Bethel lot.

We have quoted Joseph Chase Allen freely in this chapter for he was a staunch friend of Austin Tower, always showing a keen interest in the Bethel. He understood the Bethel work as well as the sailor. The following is a poem from his pen,

Service at Marine Hospital. Eleanor Tower at portable organ

and gives a pen picture of the round of little things that make up the work of the chaplain.

The Bethel Chaplain

He's a live, two fisted preacher
  That's peculiar to the coast,
Where he leads a life amphibious
  In the service of the Host.

With his Bible and his boathook,
  With his hymnal and his oar,
He makes known to fellow-mortals
  What the Lord has launched them for.

When the days and nights are pleasant
  And the fleet holds on its course,
Then you find him in his workshop
  With his tools and cooper's horse.

But when storm clouds start to gather
   And the schooners seek the lee,
Then down harbor goes the chaplain
   To bring converts in from sea.

And he brings them in his chapel,
   Built a stone's throw from the tide,
Where he works with axe and hammer
   And with book and bell beside.

Here he caulks the butts and garboards
   In the seamen's leaky souls,
And he lays the course and bearings
   For their run across the shoals.

He's a fighter, a mechanic;
   He's a painter and a scribe;
He's a coastguard and a leader
   Of the 'longshore, coastwise tribe.

For the tools of all professions
   Must come handy to his hand,
This sky-pilot of the breakers
   And the sea along the land.

Who with sailorman and fisher
   Keeps a faithful watch and ward,
While he's serving double watches
   In the charthouse of the Lord.

--Joseph Chase Allen

Through the years he was recognized as one of the Island clergy. He was secretary and treasurer of the Ministerial Association when this writer was pastor of Trinity

Methodist Episcopal Church, Oak Bluffs, in 1939-1943. He had held that position many years before and was active in that Association until his retirement. He presented the Bethel message to many congregations on the Island, and could fill a pulpit when an emergency arose.

During his years at the Bethel, Chaplain Tower experienced many storms, including the hurricanes of 1938, 1944 and 1945. The following description, by Mr. Allen, of the conditions experienced during one of these storms, is typical of many.

Austin Tower in the Bethel office

"Chaplain Tower stuck to the ship like a good captain, although the tide rose until it flooded the basement, and rising still higher, lay five inches deep or more over the main deck in the assembly room. The chimney fell and boats drifted up almost to the main gangway...Chaplain Tower did not leave his post at all that night, and was on the job cleaning up and starting repairs on the following day...but it will require a rigging crew to put the Bethel in shape for her winter voyage."

Austin had his share of accidents and sickness, and in later years several periods of illness. Below is an unusual account, again by Mr. Allen.

"Chaplain Tower of the Seaman's Bethel is back home from the hospital, refitted for resumption of service. Austin has been drydocked for some time, and according to his own report, must have been practically rebuilt from the bends on up. New fastenings, caulking of the garboard seams, new timbers, new sheathing and a general overhauling of hull and rigging; that is what the whole report amounted to. Right now he has to reeve off new running rigging and provision ship, after which he promises to go out and log off fourteen knots with a fair tide."

An event that stirred much interest took place in the Bethel in January, 1940, when Captain Zebulon Tilton of the schooner, Alice S. Wentworth, was married to Mrs. Grace McDonald of Fairhaven, Massachusetts. The ceremony was performed by Rev. William Bath, pastor of the Christ Methodist Church, Vineyard Haven.

Previous to the wedding Austin Tower, Henry A. Ritter and Philip Horton, banked the front of the Bethel with green boughs, and added a festive touch with white streamers and silver wedding bells. Captain Tilton had said he would not be married except at the wheel of his vessel. Accordingly, the wheel was removed from the Alice Wentworth, and placed in a fitting spot among the decorations.

The Bethel was crowded long before the hour set and late comers pressed against the windows for a view of the ceremony. So great was the crowd that it was half an hour before tables could be set up for the reception. According to the Vineyard Gazette account, the bride cut a huge wedding cake with a bayonet provided by the chaplain when a proper knife could not be secured.

The steamer Nantucket arrived just in time for Captain James Sandsbury and his crew to attend the service. After returning to the steamer, three blasts of the ships whistle were heard as a salute to the newly married couple.

Chaplain Tower was always ready with a helping hand

whenever a need existed. Many such instances were far beyond the call of duty. A few words should be included here regarding Dave Noble.

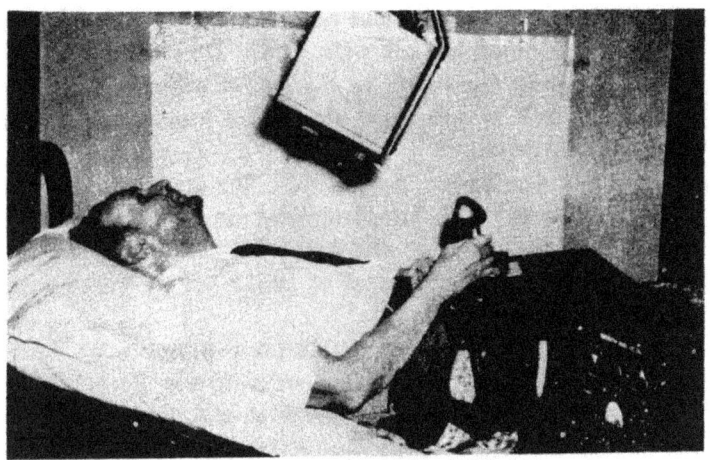

Dave Noble and his ham radio set

As a young man Dave was a patient at the Marine Hospital suffering from arthritis on his feet and knees. He was often taken to the Bethel where he enjoyed visiting with people, and at other times visited the Tower home. He enjoyed being a part of this family, and Helen was always "mom" to him. Later, as arthritis spread to other parts of his body, he was confined more closely to the hospital. When the Marine Hospital was closed in 1952, he refused to be moved to Chelsea with other chronic patients. Instead he moved from one nursing home to another. When Austin found him on a second floor, unable to get outside, he, living alone at this time, took Dave into his home. There was a large porch for his enjoyment, and Austin built a ramp over the porch steps. A first floor room was furnished with a hospital bed and other conveniences, and cared for him. At this time he could be helped out of bed, with some difficulty, and could sit only on a high bar stool because of the stiffness of his body. In time Dave's sister was able to come and care for him. His radio equipment was suspended over his bed and he became a well known ham operator. Through this and his cheerful disposition he had a wide circle of friends. He outlived both the chaplain and his sister, and was then lovingly cared for by his brother, James and his wife, Ruth. Dave always talked about "keeping the light" in the Bethel cemetery lot, but because of lack of space, he was buried beside his faithful sister, not far from it.

From the Sea Breeze, April 1950: "We are proud of what Captain Tower, our Superintendent at Vineyard Haven Bethel, has done and is still doing for Seaman Noble. He certainly deserves a great deal of credit for the part he has played in Mr. Noble's life."

Austin and his wife were very devoted to their work, never complaining though they often were at the Bethel seven nights a week and busy days which gave them limited time for family activities. When the weather was good, and the winds fair for the coastwise shipping, duties were not so pressing, time was found for the family. There were long walks to Innisfail for mayflowers or daisies; there were picnics at south beach, Indian Hill, in nearby woods or in the boat. It was an extra treat when Austin joined the children for coasting in Cat Hollow, or down the main street hill; or skating at the Mink Meadows, or Uncle Seth's Pond. On a rare evening at home there might be a fire in the fireplace for toasting marshmallows, or singing around the piano. The children also enjoyed the times when Austin tuned up his old fiddle, and played some of the old barn dance tunes which he played in his younger days.

Perhaps the best examples of the "round of little things" are the following, taken from his diary.

--Took apples to patients at Marine Hospital.
--Went out at 6:00 A.M. to look for overdue boat.
--Dug grave and buried sailor.
--Carried seaman to hospital at 5:00 A.M.
--Stayed up all night with sick sailor in fo' castle.

—Helped boy on barge get his money.
—Made fudge for sailors attending meeting.
—Went with M...to help him secure marriage license.
—Went to court on behalf of B....
—Painted town flag pole.
—Tapped and repaired shoes for sailor low on cash.
—Carried pudding to homesick boy in Marine Hospital.
—Pulled Mrs. G...'s tooth.
—Spent most of day buying clothes for wrecked seamen.
—Sick seaman phoned at 2 A.M. Spent night with him.
—Cleaned and repaired oil stove for poor old Mrs. G...
—Went to Noman's Land to bring injured boy to doctor.

End of the year notations:

1932. "Thank God for another years work. His blessings to me have been many. Good health and many boys interested in the better life."

1950. "God has been good to me this past year. 'Bless the Lord, oh, my soul, and forget not all his benefits.' May God give us peace among men in 1951."

---

[1]On Nov. 13, 1942, the Lillian E. Kerr was sunk five miles off Cape Cod with the loss of all on board. She sank within two minutes after colliding with a steamer. Six of the seven members of the crew were members of the "Hold Fast" brotherhood. Capt. J. L. Publicover was not aboard, but he lost a son and son-in-law.

Schooner Lilliam E. Kerr sunk Friday Nov 13, 1942

Chapter Thirty-Four

HOMEWARD BOUND

July 14, 1950, the Boston Seaman's Friend Society honored him upon the completion of fifty years as the "guiding skipper" of the Vineyard Haven Bethel. Following a lobster dinner, served at the Mansion House, tributes were paid the honored guest by many speakers. Joseph Chase Allen, one of Austin's warm friends who has been quoted many times in this volume, was toastmaster. He was unreserved in the praise he bestowed upon the chaplain in his own entertaining way. Words of appreciation were spoken by Rev. Orin Dice, Executive Secretary of the Society. Rev. Ralph Christie, president, spoke feelingly of the work accomplished by Mr. Tower, after which he presented a beautiful decorated plaque expressing the sincere appreciation of the Society for his years of devoted service. He was also the recipient of a check. Perhaps that which brought the greatest happiness to him was that this was the first time all of his children and grandchildren were present.

Following the dinner an open house was held at the Bethel and many townspeople gathered to offer their congratulations. Refreshments were served by the ladies from Christ Methodist Church.

Austin Tower retired June 1, 1957 after fifty seven years of service. Again a lobster dinner was served on flower bedecked tables in the banquet room of the Mansion House, and was followed by words of praise by an array of speakers.

He was feted and congratulated. They praised him for his valiant work, his sacrifice and his dangerous missions. They meant it; they were sincere; but few knew what this fifty-seven years of service really involved, for they were not seamen. Those who were present when his father-in-law passed away thirty years before, understood, for most of them knew the sea and had worked with the chaplains from the beginning. But things were different in 1957.

Austin Tower had faced both wind and sea that wrecked and killed, yet never once did he turn back when men were still in danger. He had worked his launch through cakes of ice that would have ripped holes in a much stronger vessel, if piloted by one who lacked his ability. He spent hours at night, caring for shipwrecked men who were often half frozen and physically injured, and he never left them until their needs were met.

There was no five o'clock quitting time at the Bethel. Neither was there a guarantee of a full night's sleep. This was not a life for one who craved ease or sought glory; it was a job for committed men. This was Austin Tower, a man now being honored by those who loved and knew him for his sacrifices for the men of the sea. It was beautifully done, and no one deserved the praise more than he.

Those taking part on this occasion were Sumner Johnson, in charge of arrangements, Revs. Richard P. Carter, master of ceremonies, Ralph Christie and Herman Van Lunen, chaplain from Boston. The Rev. Thomas Lehman, rector of Grace Episcopal Church, and Mrs. Wilfred White, introduced as the best qualified Vineyarder to speak, represented the Island people. Another scroll was presented on this occasion by Chauncey S. Stevens, president of the Society.

TO AUSTIN R. TOWER
FOR 57 YEARS OF LOYAL AND DEVOTED SERVICE
AS CHAPLAIN OF THE BETHEL AT VINEYARD HAVEN
FRIEND TO SEAMEN IN DISTRESS
CONSECRATED CITIZEN OF VINEYARD HAVEN
FAITHFUL SERVANT OF OUR LORD

PRESENTED BY THE DIRECTORS OF THE BOSTON SEAMAN'S FRIEND SOCIETY IN GRATEFUL APPRECIATION

In response Austin stated that he found it difficult to speak he was so filled by the tributes paid him. Then he did what he had always done, praised his father-in-law. "Mr. Edwards was a wonderful man of God," he concluded, "He was truly a fisher of men."

After the conclusion of his remarks all present stood and heartily applauded this man who was called "the sailor's best friend." He was then designated by the Society, "Chaplain Emeritus" of the local Bethel.

* * * * *

Retirement didn't come easy. The Bethel was his life and he couldn't stay away from it. On the occasion of the above, he was asked what he would do now. He replied, "If I hear a whistle blow on the waterfront, I'll probably be out of bed and down there to see what's going on." He meant it. Every day he made his usual rounds, sitting for a while at his desk in the little office, repairing or painting anything needing attention, talking with visitors or old-timers of the days gone by, then reluctantly returning home. Those who knew him best could not help notice his gradual decline. He was cheerful in conversation, but in his heart he felt a loss.

These remarks are from the Gazette. "Now the time has come for him to fold his desk in the tiny office and pass out of the gangway to become just another citizen...He sits rather sadly among the familiar things, much of which represents the work of his hands. The cabinets, bookcases, shelves, even the shingles on the buildings and the paint that covers them are his work. It was he who kept the Helen May, the Aransas and the Madison Edwards in repair. There was not much he couldn't do, and anything broken whether on an engine, a child's toy, or a bit of carpentry, he knew what needed to be done, and did it."

He gradually failed in strength. During this time he

depended more and more upon his daughter-in-law, Teresa Tower, whom the Society had hired some years before as caretaker and hostess at the Bethel. She lived in an upstairs apartment and kept things running smoothly. Austin loved his home on Mt. Aldworth, partly built by him before his marriage to Helen in 1908, and insisted that was where he would stay. As he was alone, Tessie kept watch over him, attending to his many little needs. Alden and his wife, Marcia, also came to the Vineyard when possible to be with him.[1]

The chaplain had been in the hospital for a "check-up," but suddenly on the morning of the day he was to go home, May 12, 1961, God called him. He was eighty-one.

His death sent a "shock wave through the entire island." People who knew him, admired him for his strength of character and noble deeds. They could not forget his fifty-seven years of sacrifice for the men of the sea and his interest in everyone, young or old. He was fond of children and a real friend to the many who played along the waterfront. They came to him with cut feet and scraped knees, as well as battered boats and tangled fish lines. He enjoyed tending to their little emergencies, and always stood and watched, with a smile, as they went happily on their way. Hundreds mourned him for he was a friend of all, and his helping hand was always extended to those in need.

Funeral services were held at the Christ Methodist Church, of which he had been a faithful member for many years, giving liberally of his time and service. Rev. Ralph A. Christie, acting executive of the Boston Seaman's Friend Society, officiated at the service. Following he was buried in Oak Grove cemetery beside his wife, Helen, within sight of the Bethel lot. There stands the lighthouse, built by him as a memorial to the seamen resting there. To many it will also remain a lasting memorial to the two Bethel Chaplains.

---

[1] Austin Tower's family is, and always will be, most grateful for, and appreciative of all that was done for him during these difficult years.

Chapter Thirty-Five

THE END OF AN ERA

With Austin Tower's death an exciting era had ended. The vessels with their sailor boys were gone; the Bethel boats were no more; the chaplains and their wives had departed. The Bethel they served stood as a monument to the past—a past which could never return.

In 1935 the Society felt the pinch of the depression, and wondered if the work at Vineyard Haven warranted the expense of maintaining it. When word of their discussions reached the Vineyard, the Island people were in an uproar. Herbrt N. Hinckley, who was then county treasurer, sent the committee this message "The Bethel is an institution for the greatest good, of any that the Island has ever known." Letters poured in from everywhere.

Captain Alvin B. Wasson, at that time living in Maine, wrote a letter to Boston in which he said, "This Society is very much needed to make better people and sailors out of us all. We should hate to see the time when Vineyard Haven Bethel was no more."

Letters of protest appeared in the Vineyard Gazette. Professor C. Harrison Dwight wrote, "The news of a possible cessation of the Seaman's Bethel activities is very disturbing, both to heart and soul. It wouldn't be the Vineyard without the Bethel and its work. It has been the labors of such saintly men as Madison Edwards that have kept this rotten world from destroying itself." This was the feeling of all and the Bethel was allowed to remain.

Then the unexpected happened and calmed the troubled waters for awhile. Mrs. Harriet Norris Eaton Goldberg, who for a period of years lived in the 1785 house across the street from the Bethel, had become so aware of the work being done, that in appreciation of its devoted chaplain, left in her will a sum of money, the income from which was to be used for maintaining the work of the Vineyard Haven Bethel.

After some months of deliberation the Society presented a plan that proved satisfactory to most. The building would be enlarged to include a chapel with a beautiful stained glass window, to be dedicated to the memory of Madison Edwards; and the reading room turned into a museum, in memory of Austin Tower. It soon became a tourist attraction, and hundreds visited it yearly.

The present Museum and Chapel

Now came another dedication--the last. It was observed in the lovely chapel on June 15, 1965. The organ prelude, played by Miss Sydna White, daughter of Mrs. Wilfred White, consisted of the hymns the sailors had sung at the Bethel for the last seventy-three years. The organ, a hundred and fifty years old, was presented to the Bethel as a gift of the three daughters of Captain George W. Eldridge: Mrs. Wilfred O. White, Mrs. Paul G. Macy and Mrs. Milton Harrington.

Those taking part were the Rev. Roger P. Cleveland, chairman of the Board of Governors, The Rev. Thomas H. Campbell, president of the Society, and the Rev. Carl F.

Shultz, D. D., chairman of the special committee. The key to the building was presented to the people of the Island and the Society by Rev. Richard P. Carter, and accepted by Mr. Walter R. Martin, interim Executive Director. A luncheon was served at the Mansion House.

Mrs. Osborne Tower, known to all as Tessie, began assisting Chaplain Tower in 1950. She knew the Bethel and her father-in-law as well as anyone of the family. She was loyal to him and was never at a loss for words when she felt someone was taking advantage of him. The Society respected her judgment and accepted her criticism. They also knew she was equally as anxious to offer praise when it was due, and it came as no surprise when she was made hostess of the new building.

Mrs. Osborne Tower, hostess of the new building

Once again a decision had to be made, and one that opened old wounds. The Bethel, together with adjoining property, was sold to the Steamship Authority, and now the question was would the new chapel and museum be demolished? Would it be moved to a new location? Speculation was high. The sale of the property for an expanded ferry terminal was unanimously opposed by the Island's Selectmen's Association, but was praised by many merchants. For months, ideas pro and con were exchanged, but it was too late. The Boston Society was not as indifferent as many seemed to believe. They had listened before, and now listened again. Their decision was to leave the Bethel where it was, and continue to pay the necessary expense to keep it open.

Perhaps a letter written to the Gazette by the author's wife at the time, illustrates the feeling of the family. More than any one else, this family knew what the Bethel really meant to seamen and others who had felt its influence.

"It may be a coincidence--or maybe have a deeper significance--that during this year when my husband and I have been researching diaries, journals, and old letters to glean facts for a book on the story of the Bethel and its devoted workers, that the destruction of the Bethel building should be so glibly tossed off many a tongue. We have gained even a deeper appreciation of these people since delving into the personal accounts and testimonies which they, and many others have left for our enlightment. Numerous letters from around the world are in our possession, expressing gratitude for such a place as the Bethel, where lonely sons have found friends and a homelike atmosphere; the sick assisted in getting medical help; the shipwrecked cared for; clothing supplied when needed; and for those dear ones involved in tragedy far from home, an appropriate burial and resting place with other seamen in the shadow of the lighthouse on the Bethel cemetery lot.

"We of the family as well as others who involved themselves in this service to seamen, feel the Bethel should remain, not only as a memorial to its two devoted chaplains, but just as much a memorial to the seamen it served."

The end of an era had come. Some day in the future there may remain no evidence that a mission ever existed on this spot--a spot once so sacred not only to its chaplains, but to thousands of seamen who found new life because this "House of God" was there to receive them.

AFTERWORD

In 1919, Professor Warren W. Adams was choir director of the church I attended in Boston, holding the same position at the Martha's Vineyard Campmeeting Association at Oak Bluffs. That summer he invited his choir to sing at the Association tabernacle. While there, the Bethel was one of the places we visited, meeting both chaplains at the time. Being a teenager, and not yet called to the ministry, my main interest as I recall was the curio case. There was a life preserver from the Titanic, dinner ware from another wreck, and many items contributed by sailors, brought from ports around the world, or carved by them during spare time on shipboard. Little did I know then of the devoted lives of these chaplains; and Chaplain Edwards, the humble man that he was, never dreamed that some day this active, gangling youth, would write the story of his life. Neither could Chaplain Tower imagine that this same youth would in time become his son-in-law. God indeed moves in a mysterious way.

But back to the Bethel of 1978. How changed is this "House of God" since that visit in 1919. Even though it still stands on the same site--now a combination museum and chapel, and faithful Tessie Tower smilingly welcomes the many daily visitors--in a very real sense it is deserted. No longer are heard the salty but sincere talks of the late chaplains, or the ringing voices of the seamen as they heartily sing the old hymns dear to their hearts. The only person kneeling in prayer is the occasional tourist who feels the need to approach God's altar, in the beautiful little chapel, recently added to the main building. The little office from which hundreds went forth to live a new and more meaningful life, is no more. It is now a clean modern rest room. Oh, the building, inside and out is beautiful and the Boston Seaman's Friend Society is commended for making it such, even though they no longer own it. I believe that they will agree with this writer, that as attractive as it is, the soul had gone out of it.

Of course it had to happen. It may happen in Boston and other coastal cities some day. Devotedly they still work on as those who ministered in Vineyard Haven once did. However, ships and men change. Modern methods have greatly reduced the number of seamen and dock hands. The demise of the Bethel began when the coastal sailing vessels began leaving the Vineyard to return no more. Even the barges and tugs which were once so numerous, have largely disappeared. With their going, "the home away from home" was no longer needed.

Yet it is a hallowed place. Madison Edwards and his devoted wife and family, literally wore themselves out for the men whom they loved. Austin Tower was always faithful and loving as was his gracious wife and their family.

The author preaching at the chapel

This writer preached from the pulpit in the chapel for two summers, and baptized one of his grandsons, (a great great grandson of Madison Edwards) there. Never once did he open that Bible without feeling he was standing on Holy ground. Neither of the chaplains ever stood behind that pulpit or walked in the rooms as they are now, but one can feel their presence there.

The Bible, presented to the Bethel by Helen Augusta Oliver in 1893, rests on the new pulpit. On the page in the center are recorded the names of those buried in the Bethel cemetery lot. This list is far from complete, for they ran out of space and any further records are lost.

So she stands--this lovely Bethel--a quiet oasis amidst the sound and fumes of hundreds of cars and trucks that daily board or leave the ferry. However, no matter what goes on outside, to those who know its past, the beauty and sacredness of this "House of God" is unchanging.

In preparing this book, my wife and I have spent much time over the past two years experiencing through their records and testimonies, the early, exciting days of the work of the Bethel. It seems that we have actually lived through the years of their ministry, and we cannot help but say of them, "For of such is the Kingdom of God."

ACKNOWLEDGEMENTS

Diaries, letters, newspaper accounts, the Chaplain's quarterly reports in the "Sea Breeze," (official magazine of the Boston Seaman's Friend Society), the Vineyard Gazette and the personal recollections of members of the family and others in close touch with the work, where the sources consulted.

I am also indebted to Dr. Mervin M. Deems of Brewer, Maine, Mr. Stephen Carey Luce, Jr., of Vineyard Haven, and Dr. Emory S. Bucke, former senior Editor, Abingdon Press, Nashville, Tennessee, for their interest and encouragement; The Boston Seaman's Friend Society for quotations from their official magazine, "The Sea Breeze;" Mr. Gale Huntington, vice president of Dukes County Historical Society; Mrs. Josephine Crowell, former Secretary of the Selectmen of the Town of Tisbury, for her readiness to help in securing the names of seamen interred in the Marine Hospital burial ground and the Bethel lot in Oak Grove cemetery and most important to me, the faith and encouragement of my wife, Miriam Tower Wiseman, and her help in many ways, including the typing of this manuscript.

Because so many helped the Chaplains through the years, it would be impossible to name them all. Nowhere in the world have those who worked for the interest of seamen been more generously supported than on Martha's Vineyard.

THE SEAMAN'S CEMETERIES

The most difficult part of this assignment was to secure an accurate list of names of those buried in both the Bethel lot and the Marine Hospital Cemetery. No known list exists of the Marine Hospital deaths except as they appear in the vital statistics records at the Tisbury Town Hall. Similar problems were involved in completing the Bethel list since records other than those in the Bethel Bible dating from 1898 to 1923, (and even these were definitely incomplete), were apparently lost. The following lists are therefore, far from being infallible.

Why bother with the lists at all? Because this is an important part of the history of seaman's work on Martha's Vineyard.

There were three other cemeteries in existence on the Vineyard prior to the two already mentioned. In the early years smallpox was very much a problem among seamen who inadvertently spread it to many seaport towns. To combat this threat on the Vineyard, in 1763-64 Dr. Gelston of Nantucket made regular visits to the Island for the purpose of inoculating the civilians as well as seamen. He used a building, a "so called hospital" for his work, and sailors and civilians who died of smallpox were believed to be buried in a plot on nearby Daggett Ave.

In 1789 the first Marine Hospital was built on the site of the present Lobster Hatchery, in the Eastville section of Oak Bluffs, and their burial ground was adjacent to it. Three interesting headstones are still standing, one dating back to 1804. The hospital was abandoned in 1824. An old fisherman lived in the building after that, and upon his death the structure was left to decay.

After 1824, certain doctors were on contract with the government to take care of sick seamen until 1879, when a marine hospital was again opened in an abandoned lighthouse adjacent to the present building.

One of these doctors on contract was Dr. William Leach,

who erected a hospital on the Edgartown-Vineyard Haven Road in 1866. He had a cemetery in connection with his work, although, no doubt, he took care of civilian needs also.

After the establishment of the Marine Hospital in 1879, land was purchased for a cemetery some distance away. In 1895 the hospital was moved to its present structure. From 1893 to 1898 Chaplain Edwards buried his dead in this cemetery.

It seems impossible to delve into matters of this nature without uncovering at least one mystery. In the Bethel Bible appears the name of a sailor who died in 1906 and was buried in the Bethel lot; we found his stone there. Yet of the few headboards still standing and readable in the Marine Hospital cemetery, is the name of the same man including identical information. The headboard is still firmly set, but whose resting place does it mark?

BETHEL CEMETERY LOT

	Name	Age	Place of birth	Date of Death	Cause of Death
1.	Unknown		Body washed ashore	11-26-98	'98 Storm
2.	Unknown		Body washed ashore	11-26-98	'98 Storm
3.	William McElweis	46	New Brunswick	11-29-98	'98 Storm
4.	Karl Wm. Larsen	20	Denmark	8-12-99	Fall from aloft
5.	Andrew Suri	45	Greece	7- 6-00	Heart Failure
6.	Unknown		Italy	7- 7-00	At sea
7.	Albin Anderson	19	Sweden	1-23-02	Enteric fever
8.	Cornelius Giessen	27	Holland	11-23-02	Fall from aloft
9.	James Finde	23	West Indies	5-31-03	Bullet in lungs
10.	Henry Olsen	32	Sweden	5-28-04	Wood alcohol
11.	Unknown		Body washed ashore, Naushon	7-19-04	
12.	Niels Hanson	18	Norway	9-25-04	Fell in hole
13.	Unknown		Body washed ashore Herring Creek	6- 3-05	
14.	John A. Carlsen	33	Sweden	12-24-05	Fall from aloft
15.	William Reddick	44		8-30-06	Heart disease
16.	Albin Olsen	22	Sweden	7-21-06	Injuries
17.	William Smith	25	Virginia	9- 2-06	Acc. drowning
18.	John Oskall	52	Finland	11-28-06	Caught in steam wench
19.	Andrew Anderson	42	Sweden	1-17-07	Suicide

20.	Gustav Gunner Mannerstrom	29	Finland	-07	Pneumonia
21.	Charles Hughes	35		1-23-09	Suffocation - coal gas
22.	Gorth Larson	27	Sweden	1-28-10	Brain tumor
23.	James Williams	82	England	4-26-10	Grippe
24.	Otto Yanson	24	Finland	4-25-10	Fracture, Skull, fall
25.	Andrew Carlson	64	Finland	12-26-10	Fracture, Skull, Fall
26.	Richard Halstead	19	Denmark	3-24-11	Frozen at sea
27.	Unknown	Washed ashore		3-24-11	
28.	Unknown	Washed ashore		8-28-11	
29.	Gilman C. Colson	54		3-15-12	Amputation
30.	Edward Jensen	66		11-18-12	Acc. drowning
31.	Albert Weagle			12- 5-12	Congest. lungs
32.	Clinton Grove	16		8- 2-13	Tuberculosis
33.	Johan Anton Johnson	64	Sweden	9- 8-13	Pleurisy
34.	Barney Forstad	37	Norway	2- 9-14	Heart disease
35.	Nels Sognstad	24	Norway	3-20-14	Cancer
36.	Hans Hansen	53	Denmark	10-24-14	Cereb. hem.
37.	Martin Yearsen	52	Denmark	12-25-14	Stroke
38.	Fred McLaughlin	22	Nova Scotia	6-21-15	Acc. drowning
39.	Antin Anderson	23	Denmark	-16	Not given
40.	Bjorne Forstad	22	Norway	-16	Not given
41.	Henry Thorndale	30	Mexico	4-13-17	Tuberculosis
42.	Charles Cooper	60		10- 6-18	Heart disease
43.	Unknown	Washed ashore		10- 3-19	
44.	Unknown	Washed ashore Cuttyhunk		7-25-20	
45.	James J. Murfee	58		11-23-21	Heart disease
46.	Charles Gadeyne	21	Holland	12-14-22	Heart disease
47.	Harry King	31	New York	4-16-23	Acc. drowning
48.	Warren Bray	21	Maine	10- 4-23	Tuberculosis
49.	Charles A. Olsen	50	Sweden	10- 3-25	Spticemia
50.	Unknown	Washed ashore off Hedge Fence		7-22-26	
51.	William Fults	51		6-15-28	Tuberculosis
52.	Ludwig Arnesen	50		3-14-29	Hemorrhage
53.	Manuel Corey	41	Cape Verde	9-20-29	Heart disease
54.	Edgar H. Austry	58		5-27-32	Cereb. hem.
55.	Alfred Eskedahl	54	Sweden	3- 6-34	
56.	Frank A. Hamilton	60		12- 6-34	Tbc. and heart
57.	Charles A.Wallace			9-12-35	Drowning
58.	Robert Zwicker	63	Nova Scotia	2-15-36	Cancer, bladder
59.	Peter Fernandez	57	Spain	5-27-37	Heart
60.	Kurt Diethert	35	Germany	8-15-37	Fracture, spine
61.	Benjamin Almeida	39	Spain	8-31-37	
62.	Johnson Martin	53	Norway		
63.	Crobin Welsh	22		7-20-38	Acc. drowning
64.	Louis Desjardins	56	France	1- 7-39	
65.	Dewey Stevenson	71	Denmark	3-17-39	Diabetes
66.	John Forrestal	66	Newfoundland	11-30-40	Heart
67.	Unknown	Washed ashore,		12-23-40	

	Name	Age	Place of birth	Date of Death	Cause of Death
68.	Ernest Goodick	63	No Man's Land Nova Scotia	6-14-41	Hypertension
69.	Perry Robbins	51	Maine	2-28-43	Heart
70.	Charles Hamilton	77		12-23-45	Heart
71.	Wiano Mattila	51	Finland	2- 3-46	Cereb. Hem.
72.	Patrick King	65	Ireland	9-21-46	Pneumonia
73.	Selma Brandesborg	63	Norway	6-29-49	Heart

MARINE HOSPITAL CEMETERY

	Name	Age	Place of birth	Date of Death	Cause of Death
1.	Manuel P. Delgarde	35	Cape Verde	1-28-88	Heart disease
2.	Levi Williams	37	Maine	4-20-88	Malaria, nephritis
3.	Martin Hansen	23	Norway	7-21-89	Typhoid fever
4.	John Antone	22		8-15-89	Consumption
5.	William Nathan	48	England	11-25-89	Pneumonia
6.	Carl Loderburg	29	Finland	1-14-90	Broken leg, hemorrhage
7.	James Riley	29		4-22-90	Pneumonia
8.	John McGregor	48	Scotland	6-16-90	Abdominal aneurism
9.	Higgins Carey	54		9- 8-90	Not given
10.	Peter Santos	43	Philippines	12-25-90	Tuberculosis
11.	Michael Moran	33	Penn.	4- 2-91	Tuberculosis
12.	James Madison	52	Rhode Island	5-20-91	Influenza
13.	Jose Gomes Sevena	19	Cape Verde	5-30-91	Tuberculosis
14.	Albion Alley	58		6-10-91	Emphysema
15.	John McGuire	24		8-23-91	Enteric fever
16.	Albert Henrickson	25	Finland	11-12-91	Accident at sea
17.	Edward Prior	22	New Jersey	6-27-92	Erysipelas
18.	James Morrisey	30		8-24-92	Beri-beri
19.	James Muise	25	Nova Scotia	9-10-92	Typhoid fever
20.	Karl Peterson	22	Norway	5-25-93	Tuberculosis
21.	Stephen Walruth	55	New York	9-23-93	Dysentery
22.	Frank Smith	41	Belgium	8-16-94	Bright's disease
23.	David Smith	62		4-23-94	Ruptured blood vessel of heart
24.	Thomas T. Page	24		7-27-94	Enteric fever
25.	Jacob Doornbos	45	Holland	2- 9-96	Not given
26.	Frank W. Eastman	50		4-22-96	Amputation, stroke
27.	John La Pore	58	New York	6-23-96	Remittent fever
28.	John McDonald	20	Prince Ed. Is.	1-10-96	Enteric fever
29.	Rudolph Rolfson	21	Norway	1-27-97	Skull fracture
30.	C. A. Foster			12-24-98	Heart Attack
31.	Unknown		Body washed ashore	9-21-98	
32.	Unknown		Body washed ashore	9-23-98	
33.	Unknown		Body washed ashore	9-23-98	
34.	S. M. Norwood		Body washed ashore	9-27-98	
35.	Unknown		Body washed ashore	11-29-98	
36.	Unknown		Body washed ashore	11-29-98	

#	Name	Age	Origin	Date	Cause
37.	Unknown		Body washed ashore	12-2-98	
38.	William Johnson	30		1-10-98	Arsenic poisoning
39.	Manuel Pena	22		1-11-99	Tuberculosis
40.	John McLeod	61	Ireland	4-22-99	Cancer
41.	William O. Adams	45		7-22-99	Heart failure
42.	Englebert Kordlein	47		10-16-99	Not given
43.	Alfred Smith	23		12-8-99	Beri-beri
44.	John Wheaton	41		8-20-00	Enteric fever
45.	Samuel Williams	23		12-8-00	Heart disease
46.	Edward W. Forrester	50		6-20-02	Pneumonia
47.	Richard Lewis	25		10-10-02	Tuberculosis
48.	John Boy	50	Cuba	10-13-02	Tuberculosis
49.	Henry Hussey	76		1-17-04	Cerebral Hem.
50.	James Duffy	60	Ireland	5-22-05	Degen. spinal cord
51.	Thomas Warren	60	Nova Scotia	12-29-05	Cirrhosis liver
52.	Joseph Myers	46	Germany	5-28-06	Head injury
53.	Robert J. Topley	58		10-4-10	Heart attack
54.	James McIntosh	34		12-5-12	Gangrene
55.	George Jensen	38	Denmark	8-31-13	Burns
56.	Ole A. Olson	62	Norway	2-14-14	Stroke
57.	Robert Gastfins	68		5-22-14	Stroke
58.	Oscar Harvey	23	Alabama	3-19-15	Pneumonia
59.	Samuel Lucke	58	Denmark	6-21-15	Heart disease
60.	Fred Tarruttie	53	Germany	12-27-15	Nephritis
61.	John L. Gustavson	58	Sweden	4-19-16	Bright's disease
62.	William Black	41		10-15-16	Diabetes
63.	John Lopes	49	Cape Verde	1-16-17	Hemiplegia
64.	Manuel Taves	45	Cape Verde	7-24-18	Cirrhosis, liver
65.	John McInnis	30	Scotland	10-6-18	Pneumonia
66.	Julius Jergensen	67	Denmark	12-27-18	Heart disease
67.	Joseph Smith	23	Alabama	3-3-23	Tuberculosis
68.	Christian Neilsen	22	Denmark	6-30-20	Nephritis
69.	Olaf Edwards	46	Norway	12-27-23	Nephritis
70.	Cornelis Visser	37	Holland	11-23-25	Sudden death
71.	Olaf Aas	24	Norway	7-16-26	Tuberculosis
72.	Fred E. Whittemore	64		1-1-27	Pneumonia
73.	Henry F. Flemming	56		5-23-27	Heart disease
74.	Randolph Louis	29		2-7-28	Pyemia
75.	George F. Harris	58		10-4-31	Nephritis
76.	Juan Echevaria	37	Spain	5-31-37	Tuberculosis

www.ingramcontent.com/pod-product-compliance
Lightning Source LLC
Chambersburg PA
CBHW031348040426
42444CB00005B/230